וַיֵּצֶא ...שֶׁר מִשָּׁרָשָׁיו יִפְרֶה

The RABBI From BURBANK

Isidor Zwirn *and* Bob Owen

וַיֵּצֵא חֹטֶר מִגֶּזַע יִשָׁי וְנֵצֶר מִשָּׁרָשָׁיו יִפְרֶה

The RABBI From BURBANK

Isidor Zwirn *and* Bob Owen

KENNETH

COPELAND

PUBLICATIONS

The royal line of David will be cut off, chopped down like a tree; but from the stump will grow a Shoot—yes, a new Branch from the old root.

Isaiah 11:1

Foreword

Through the years, my interest and love for Judaism has grown. *The Rabbi From Burbank* so deeply touched my life, I sought to bring it back into print.

Ken and I have preached the integrity of God's Word and putting God's Word first for more than 35 years now. Ken and I are not Hebrew scholars, though our love for and commitment to the Word of God transcends all other things in our lives. This book is a window into Jewish education...not only is every Word of Torah valued, but every letter of every Word is studied as it is in reality, the very Word of Jehovah.

Reading *The Rabbi From Burbank* was a continual discovery of common ground with the Jewish faith. In the text, I found the basic roots of our belief system: the integrity of the Word, the awareness and guidance of the Holy Spirit, love for family, deep commitment to instill in our children the Word of God, the separateness of God's people, hunger for the truth and reverence for the names of God, to name a few. We in fact hold dear the very same patriarchs of the faith, such as Abraham, Moses and David.

The personal triumph of a persecuted boy and his courage as an adult to objectively follow where his study of Torah led him, I believe, will correct many misconceptions and may change your life forever. Shalom.

Gloria Copeland

The Rabbi From Burbank

ISBN 1-57562-729-9   30-0813

08 07 06 05 04   6 5 4 3 2

Kenneth Copeland Publications

Fort Worth, Texas 76192-0001

For more information about Kenneth Copeland Ministries, call
1-800-600-7395 or visit www.kcm.org.

וַיֵּצֵא חֹטֶר מִגֶּזַע יִשָׁי וְנֵצֶר מִשָּׁרָשָׁיו יִפְרֶה

CONTENTS

T O R A H   I S . . .

A tree of life to those who take hold
of her, Long life is in her right hand; In
her left hand are riches and honor. Her
ways are pleasant ways, And all
her paths lead to peace.

וַיֵּצֵא חֹטֶר מִגֵּזַע יִשָׁי וְנֵצֶר מִשָׁרָשָׁיו יִפְרֶה

CHAPTER ONE
TRAINED IN TORAH

The Sabbath began as usual at our Orthodox synagogue until I stepped up to the *bimah,* the platform, to read the weekly portion from the Torah. Then pandemonium broke loose. Before I really knew what was happening, two huge uniformed police officers suddenly appeared, grabbed me by both arms, and started moving me toward the doorway.

"What's happening? What are you doing?" I asked, more startled than angry.

"Just come along quietly, Rabbi," one of the officers said. "We're leaving the synagogue."

"But, why? I belong here. I'm one of the rabbis. I don't understand..."

"Let's go," he said, tightening his grip on my arm.

"But..."

The pressure on my arms increased. "C'mon, Rabbi. Let's go."

I couldn't believe what was happening. For one wild moment I wondered if this was how it had happened in Germany. I looked at the congregants, hoping that they would do something, that they would rescue me from these officers. But they just looked at me, most of them with startled looks on their faces. Not a single one of them raised a hand or voice to help me.

Within moments we were off the *bimah*, down the aisle, and out on the street. As soon as the officers released their grip on my arms, I turned to reenter the synagogue. Immediately, they grabbed me again. "Sorry, Rabbi, but you can't go back in there."

"But, I don't understand," I said. "This is the Sabbath. I came here to worship. Why can't I be allowed to do so?"

"All I know, Rabbi," one officer said, "is that we were told to remove you from the synagogue...and to tell you not to come back again. We just did our job. That's all we know."

"But I belong in there," I protested. "I'm one of the rabbis..."

One of the huge officers towered above me, shaking his head. "Sorry, Rabbi Zwirn," he said, "but our orders were to remove you from the synagogue, which we did. And to prevent you from entering it, which we're going to do if you try to get back in. Sorry..."

The impact of the officers' words struck me full force: I had just been forcibly ousted from my own synagogue! The action was a harsh reminder to me that, as a Jew, an Orthodox Jew and a rabbi at that, my decision to become a follower of the Messiah was not being looked upon with favor by my fellow Jews.

I came from a long line of Orthodox Jews. Though my father was a *tzaddik*, a righteous man, he was not a rabbi. Nor was my paternal grandfather of blessed memory, though he was even more strict and pious than my father. With his long, white, flowing beard, dressed in his black coat and black hat, Grandfather was a very imposing person.

Because of the biblical injunction, "Thou shalt have no graven images before me," my grandfather and most Orthodox Jews traditionally have made a practice of not posing for photographs. So Grandfather would not allow any photographs to be taken of him. However, just before he went to his eternal reward, a member of our family was able to take one picture of him.

Orthodox Jewish fathers and their sons usually

develop a very close and lasting relationship. My father's and mine was no exception. Some of my earliest memories in New York City are sitting with him while we studied the weekly portion from the Torah and Haftarah (a section from the Book of Prophets).

My father wanted me to become a rabbi, just as his father had wanted him to be. For the past 2,000 years or so, any Orthodox Jew who wanted his son to become a rabbi would send him to a Hebrew school called a *yeshivah*, also called *bet hamidrash*, "house of research." The name comes from the words *bet*, meaning "house" and *doresh* which means "to seek, ask, question or research."

Before the boy can be accepted as a *yeshivah* student at the age of six, however, he must already know how to pray in Hebrew and understand what he is saying. This required level of learning can be compared to an incoming student in an American secular school having to be able to read English and also having considerable knowledge of the language.

For me to achieve this somewhat advanced level of learning by age six, my father, and all other fathers who desired to send their sons to the Yeshivah Rabbenu Yaacov Yoseph in New York City, started teaching me to read and pray from the Orthodox Prayer Book from the time I was only three years of age. That was in 1918. And as far as I know, this standard had not changed, either in the United States or Israel.

From the very first day in the *yeshivah,* our textbook was the Torah. And, of course, the Torah was in Hebrew. As each student was called upon in turn, he had to read the next sentence and give his interpretation of what the verse meant to him.

The teaching rabbi would then give his and other rabbis' interpretation of that verse, and encourage all the students to participate in the ensuing dialogue. Often this dialogue would center around the meaning of a single word in the sentence. Sometimes the meaning of the entire passage would even hinge upon a single letter of a single word. The discussions that grew out of such intense studies gave rise to the standing joke that whenever two Jews meet for a conversation, you can expect at least three or four different opinions.

Basically, that is how we studied, both in the *yeshivah* and in our homes. This method taught us love and respect for the honest opinions of others, even though they might differ or conflict with our own. This same respect for the opinions of others was expressed when we began to research the Talmud (the written record of the Oral Law and the discussion of the Sages concerning its interpretation) and other religious books that we studied.

Our learning was accompanied by a catchy tune, that no *yeshivah* child could ever forget, with the words going something like, "And so said Rabbi X...and so said Rabbi Y...and so said Rabbi Z..." and so on.

The same method of study, with the same openness in expression of personal opinions, and the same respect for the opinions of others, was adopted wherever we studied, even at home during the times when my father and I would review the weekly portion of the Torah (which is read by Jews all around the world).

We were taught, and I firmly believe it to be true, that there is no way of ever arriving at eternal truths unless all concepts and all opinions are allowed to be discussed openly. We were taught that this was the way that free men and children of the free were to study life. It could be said that this *bet hamidrash* method of study is based upon the commandment, "Thou shalt love thy neighbor as thyself."

Of course, the *bet hamidrash*, house of learning, method stands out in stark contrast to the principle adopted by many teachers, preachers, and professors who feel that they must ban all opposing views, and who say by their attitude, "In my class I allow for only one opinion or viewpoint: my own!"

We Jews sometimes like to poke fun at ourselves with funny stories. One of the most popular of these was seen in Shalom Aleichem's well-known play and motion picture, Fiddler on the Roof. The basis for Aleichem's story, as well as the anecdote, comes from the fact that, in the ghettos of Europe, the rabbis served as judges in addition to their religious duties.

In the story, Moisha and Jake came one day to the rabbi to settle a dispute. First the rabbi listened to Moisha's long complaint against Jake. When he finished, the rabbi said, "Moisha, *du bist gerecht*" ("You are right").

Then the rabbi called in Jake and listened to his viewpoint of the controversy. When he finished, the rabbi said, "Jake, *du bist gerecht*."

It seems that it is the custom for *rebbetzin*, rabbis' wives, to listen to all such complaints through the keyhole. Thus, when the discussions were over and the two men had gone, the *rebbetzin* came into the room and spoke indignantly. "They can't both be right!"

The rabbi stopped a moment to rethink his decision, then answered, "You know, *Rebbetzin*, you, too, are right."

In the Talmud it is written, "As a hammer splits

the rock into many splinters, so will a scriptural verse yield many meanings." An honest Bible scholar will inevitably realize the truth of this saying.

The *bet hamidrash* method of studying Torah may sound strange to those who are accustomed to accepting their teacher's viewpoint as final authority without personally investigating his statements. A *yeshivah* student would not necessarily agree with the divergent points of view, but he was expected to accept them as being the honest views of the ones who expressed them. Each person had to decide for himself which of the expressed viewpoints was true for him.

This *bet hamidrash* method of study would continue throughout the Sabbath in the small Bronx synagogue where my father and I attended, until just before the evening *havdalah*, the services which marked the end of the Sabbath.

Then, even though no rabbi was present, the dialogue on the weekly portions would be loudly discussed around a table heavily laden with delicious Jewish food. These discussions were hot and heavy, and to an outsider they might have appeared disorganized. Within Jewish Orthodoxy, scenes like this, portrayed in the motion picture, *Yentl,* still continue.

Being a Jewish boy in those days wasn't easy, especially where I lived. Jewish children were often the butt of crude and cruel jokes and even violence. I soon learned to stay away from *goyim*, Gentile boys or men. On more than one occasion they would catch me and treat me shamefully, sometimes burning my face with the glowing end of a cigarette. As I writhed and cried out in pain, they laughed and made slurring remarks about Jews. The first time they called me a "Christ killer," I asked my father about it.

He shook his head. "No, son, we are no more Christ killers than they are. The Romans crucified the Gentiles' Jesus, not the Jews."

Though Pops, as I always called him, was very careful in his speaking about the *goyim*, I realized that he, too, feared and perhaps even hated them. Most of the Jewish community honestly believed that all Gentiles were "Jew haters" and were to be avoided. Consequently, neither my father nor any of our Jewish friends did business with Gentiles if they could help it.

These early experiences solidified my attitudes towards the Gentiles, attitudes which continued throughout my life until recent years. It seemed to me then that Jews and Gentiles had nothing in common. It seemed that the only similarity was that we were both human. However, even at that point the Gentiles seemed to have some doubts about us, as they often called us "swine" and accused us of having horns on our heads like animals.

We dressed differently. Both Jewish men and women dressed mostly in somber black year around, while Gentiles made quite generous use of color in their dress.

We ate differently. All Jewish people I knew at that time were careful to eat kosher, which meant they had to buy their foods and meats from kosher, "clean," Jewish stores and markets. It seemed to us that Gentiles had little regard for God's commandments regarding food.

Our concept of God was different. From the time I was very young I was taught that Christians worshiped three Gods, the Father, the Son, and the Holy Spirit, instead of one Yehovah, whom the Jewish people worshiped. And the Christians worshiped on Sunday instead of on the Sabbath, the day we believed God had ordained for rest and worship.

Even our schools were different. Jewish schooling was centered around Torah, while the few Gentile children with whom I had casual contact appeared to have absolutely no regard for God's Word. In fact, they seemed to be totally ignorant of anything that had to do with God.

So, from my earliest childhood and youth, I was led to believe that Jews and Gentiles had nothing in common, and we Jews were to have nothing to do with "them."

As a Jewish boy and young man, my every awareness was of Yehovah. My thoughts were constantly centered upon the fact of his presence in my life. In the truest sense of the word, it was not just faith in his presence, but distinctly more than that. His presence was a foregone conclusion. I was aware of the *fact* of his presence.

This belief was the result of the prayers that my father taught me to pray when I awakened, before eating or drinking, and upon seeing God's wonders in the universe. Every thought and every action was inextricably connected with God's presence.

That same awareness of Yehovah was present in my *bet hamidrash* method of study and learning. I was taught that Yehovah not only cared about my learning, but that he commanded me to study and learn Torah, and the accepted method of so doing was through *bet hamidrash*.

Throughout my life I realized that in the Hebrew

language, *every letter* and *every word* is important. Every one has a meaning and a purpose. None is superfluous. Many centuries ago, a form of Jewish mysticism arose called *Kabbalah,* which gave a numerical system of interpreting Scripture. To the Kabbalist, each letter of the Hebrew alphabet has an eternal numerical value. Kabbalists have computer-like minds, with the ability to total the numerical values of each Hebrew word, sentence, and paragraph. Thus, as they study, they compare a word, sentence, or paragraph with other similar words, sentences, or paragraphs found in other parts of the Torah. This enables them to clarify the section under discussion. Therefore, what might appear to be a very difficult passage of Scripture to the average biblical student would be very simple to them.

During my early years of study, the *bet hamidrash* principles of Torah study became so deeply ingrained in me that I could never forget them. The word *Torah* usually refers to the first five books of the Bible and is often translated "the Law." It is best translated, however, as "instruction" or "teaching," God's revealed will for our lives.

To this day, I can hear the voices of my rabbis and teachers as they expounded. "Remember," they said over and over again, "Torah is our textbook. Only Torah. When we study Torah it is both our text and our commentary."

To this day, when I study the Bible, I depend upon the Bible to be its own comprehensive and reliable commentary.

וַיֵּצֵא הֲזֹר וַחֹמֶר מַגַּע יָשִׁין נָצֹר מִשְׁרָשָׁיו יְפָרוֹ

CHAPTER TWO

LOWER EAST SIDE

I have a few fuzzy remembrances of my natural mother, but the only sharp memory I have is of her funeral. I was only five when she died during one of New York City's terrible flu epidemics that followed World War I. Mom had been a very active woman. In addition to providing a home for my father, my sister, and me, Mom had a doll repair shop, all of which kept her very busy. My father was a tailor in a clothing factory.

I don't know why, but Mom was sick a lot. She was frequently in and out of hospitals. I suppose she was already weak and run down when the terrible flu epidemic in 1919 struck our heavily populated section of New York City. Anyway, within days after she contracted the flu, she was dead. After the funeral, my father, my sister, and I returned to our now empty, silent apartment. Before Mom died, we lived in a nice neighborhood in Manhattan. But soon after Mom's funeral, Pops moved his little family to the Lower East Side.

Some of my earliest remembrances are of our house there on Canyon Street, about five blocks from the East River. Several thousand Jewish families lived in this Jewish community. And, along with another family, the Zwirns lived in a rented five-story house. Five stories high and no elevator! Everything had to be carried up and down those long flights of stairs.

And since we all tired of running up and down those stairs many times a day, you would frequently hear, "Mom, throw me down a shirt..." Or, "Isidor, throw me a..."

By today's standards, living conditions there were intolerable. We had only one toilet for two families, and we could take a shower only once a week.

My grandparents lived about a dozen blocks away, and we visited them regularly. Our *shul*, synagogue, was only about three or four blocks from our home. It was small, probably not more than fifty people at the most. But it was the center of our Jewish religious and social life. My father had come from Jikev, Poland, and all of the Jews in our *shul* were also from Poland. They composed a *chevrim*, a brotherhood.

It was a true brotherhood. We cared for each other,

for both the living and the dead. If a man had a need, it was our duty as brothers to loan or give him what he needed. And when one of our number died, we tenderly laid him away in our own little burial place. We did all of this according to our Torah and our traditions.

Our Jewish court system, the *bet din,* was also enacted according to the Torah. When brothers had a complaint of any kind that they couldn't settle themselves, they brought it before the rabbis, who would handle the matter with a *bet din*. All in all, Jewish family and community life in those days was a beautiful example of how God could live his life in us and through us. We truly loved one another.

It had to be so, even as it had been across the ages, otherwise we Jews would have been decimated and wiped off the face of the globe, as Hitler and others attempted to do. Though we faced anti-Semitism even in New York City, that persecution wasn't nearly as bad as it had been in Poland and other parts of Europe, according to my father. In the United States, the government tried to quell anti-Semitism, but in parts of Europe, the government often condoned or recommended it.

In certain areas on the East Side we Jews experienced

great persecution, especially us boys. We didn't dare go to our *yeshivahs* alone because the Irish kids in the nearby communities would try to beat us up. The sound we most feared was the shout, "Here come the kikes again. Let's get them!"

They would descend upon us from every direction, yelling like wild Indians, "Christ killers! Christ killers! Here come the Christ killers!" They would surround us, hitting and kicking us. We would put our backs together, so they couldn't get behind us, and protect ourselves as well as we could until they tired of their sport or we managed to break through their ranks and get away. Their favorite sport was for several of them to hold one of us and burn our faces with the glowing ends of their cigarettes. Many young Jewish boys have been scarred in this way for life.

Though it was a hard life for Pops, trying to be both father and mother to his two orphaned children, I never heard him complain. But after two years, Pops tired of his dual role as a single parent and married my "second mother," a beautiful woman. Early in the twentieth century, the words "stepmother" carried an ugly connotation, and the rest of our family prophesied dire consequences for Pops and his children.

But none of their predictions came true. Pops and

Mom lived happily together well past their fiftieth wedding anniversary. As for my sister and me, we never thought of Mom as our stepmother, nor the two children she bore Pops as stepchildren. No natural mother could have been a better mother to us.

Everything Mom did exemplified love. And the home she made for Pops and us kids was a true Jewish home. Today, as I look at the "homes" around me, which are really little more than addresses where parents and the kids come to sleep and eat, I realize what a wonderful heritage my parents gave me.

Until I was fifteen years old, I had no social contact whatsoever with Gentiles. The *goyim* lived close to the river, and the Jews lived several blocks away. Today that part of New York is called a ghetto. Maybe the *goyim* called it a ghetto when I lived there. If they did, I didn't know it. As far as I was concerned, it was just our neighborhood, the section of the city where we Jews, in our brownstone houses, could live together in peace.

In true Jewish tradition, Pops and Mom were the patriarch and matriarch of our large family, which included all of our cousins. Whenever any member of our extended family had a problem, or whenever husbands and wives among them encountered marital difficulties, they brought them to Pops and Mom for adjudication and advice. And to my knowledge, their counsel and judgment were always successful. Stories of their involvements in the lives of the family would fill a book.

Our home was not just home. It was the Zwirn hotel, hospital, and restaurant. Anyone recuperating from an operation would do so in our home. Anyone suffering from a bad cold, the flu, or pneumonia would seek relief through the application of Mom's famous *bancas,* a Jewish remedy that seldom failed to bring relief.

And it was understood that all such advice, food, accommodations, and other services were rendered free of charge. No remuneration would be accepted. No one would dare offend Mom by offering her money.

Passover at the Zwirn home was a special occasion for the entire family. For a full week before Passover, Mom would be busy day and night preparing for this looked-forward-to feast and celebration. The largest room in the house was chosen for the *seder,* and into it was squeezed our enlarged dining table. Those who desired to participate had to come early to get a seat because no standing was allowed during this important event. Nor could there be "double shifts," as at other festivals. This joyous feast, celebrating the Israelites' deliverance from Egyptian bondage, began immediately after sundown and lasted until midnight. No family member wanted to be excluded.

How blessed was our family and community! Even then, as a young boy, despite the fact that I had been deprived of my mother and a mother's care for two years, I never lacked the love and acceptance of our community and family. Vivid memories of that love remain with me, and whenever I have undergone some of the trials and privations that come to all families, the stability and role modeling my parents provided for us children have held me steady.

Today, three score years hence, I witness the disintegration of American family life with horror. It is no wonder to me that there is so much delinquency, so great a loss of home and national values, such a breakdown in all levels of society. All this seems inevitable if there is no home and community life.

Even among the Christian homes that I have known in the past few years, have I rarely seen anything like the closely knit family life I knew as a young Jewish boy. More so than ever, I understand

God's wisdom in his promotion of family life.
Someone said, "As the home goes, goes the nation."
Though I am not sure who said this, I am certain
it is true.

The power of Torah, God's immutable Word,
was the center and source of all that we did.
As Jewish families, we studied Torah, we lived by
Torah, we talked Torah. Our lives were intimately
impacted by Torah. The way we lived, the way we
died, the way we worshiped, the way we married and
treated our wives and children, the way we conducted
business—everything we did was a reflection of our
Torah. Everything.

I have no doubt that God had this in mind when
he spoke in his Word, "Raise up a child in the way he
should go (Torah), and when he is old he will not
depart from it (Torah's way)." The truth of this statement is borne out in the lives of Jewish children. One
will rarely find a Jew who does not say, "I was born a
Jew. I will die a Jew."

The reason for this is Torah, which we all begin to
study, to learn, and to pattern our lives after at a very
early age.

CHAPTER THREE
THE BRONX—AND ON TO CALIFORNIA

When I was fifteen years old, Pops bought a
house in the Bronx, and we moved there from the
Lower East Side. In the Bronx, for the first time in my
life, I became friends with a *goy*. Tony was a Jewish
Italian, but he was as non-Jewish as he could be.
I called him a "Jewish *goy*," which may seem like a
contradiction in terms, but actually it wasn't. Though
Tony and his family were nice people, they were
totally secular and never had any contact with religion, the Bible, or tradition. Except for their Jewish
heritage, they were non-Jewish. But I liked Tony
and we became good friends.

Life in the Bronx was different than
on the East Side. I spent ten wonderful years there.

My father was instrumental in staring a *shul*
across the street from our new home. Most Orthodox

synagogues are small, and this one was no different. It occupied the second floor of a two-story apartment building. Jewish people love cantorial music. So, even though our synagogue had no rabbi, we did have a *chazan,* a cantor. Pops loved that cantor and would *daven* (pray) with him. After eating the *Shabbat* meal, the two of them would occasionally walk down to the big synagogue and listen to their beautiful cantorial music.

I will never forget our Sabbaths. The Sabbath lasted from sundown Friday evening until the appearance of the first evening star on Saturday evening, but all of Friday was lived in anticipation of the peace and beauty of our coming Sabbath.

Mom set Friday aside for *Shabbat* preparation: marketing, cleaning, and cooking. Since the Sabbath was a day of rest, all food had to be prepared the day before. The house was filled with the wondrous smells of cooking things. As the evening drew near, a serene stillness settled upon the whole community. The men hurried home from their shops and factory jobs, greeting each other with the traditional "Shabbat shalom," "Good Shabbos."

Parents and children dressed in their best for the looked-forward-to *Shabbat* meal. All across our

predominately Jewish neighborhood, the women offi-
cially welcomed the Sabbath to their homes with the
lighting of the *Shabbat* candles and their traditional
prayers: "Blessed art Thou, O Lord our God, King of the
universe, who sanctified us by his commandments
and commanded us to kindle the Sabbath light." Then
came Pops' traditional blessing over us children.

With the coming of our biblical Sabbath, it
seemed that the very peace of God himself, his *shekinah*,
fell upon us, and we rejoiced in his presence. I can
never forget the happiness and the serenity of those
Sabbaths we spent as a family. Recently, when my
sister, Shirley, and her husband came to visit us,
we reminisced for hours about those happy days of
our childhood.

For a year or so after moving to the Bronx, another
boy and I would take the train back to the *yeshivah*
and study Torah. It was a long ride, about forty minutes each way, and it soon proved to be too difficult
and time consuming, so we discontinued. However,
Pops and I continued to *daven* together and to read the
daily portion together until I married and left home.

When I was old enough, I began looking for a
job. My father was happy about that, but urged me
not to spend my lifetime working for others. "Become

independent," he told me over and over again. "Don't work for others."

Of course I had to work for someone else to begin with, so I got a job in a fur factory. Remembering Pops' words, I worked hard. I never shunned any job they gave me. Consequently, after four years I became so knowledgeable about the fur industry that I opened my own shop. Business was good, and I soon went into partnership with two well-established furriers.

During those years anti-Semitic feelings ran high, and it was next to impossible to sell to department stores if it became known you were Jewish. In fact, when I moved to California in 1947, it was common to see signs on business establishments that read, "No Jews or dogs allowed."

So, either in New York or California, if your business card gave your name as Abraham or Isaac, fur buyers would simply refuse to see you. My business associates called me Barney, a name that some of my friends still call me. Though I wasn't ashamed of my Jewishness, I had to live, so when I had business cards printed, they read, "Barney Zwirn."

I was about twenty-four years of age and doing well in business when I met Rae, the woman who was to become my wife. We met at Rockland Lake, where a number of Jewish families had summer bungalows. We were attracted to each other, fell in love, and a year later were married. Since both of us had Orthodox backgrounds, we had no religious disagreements and we peaceably began our lives together.

Despite my good intentions, though, after marriage, the grim realities of making a living during those Depression years put a temporary halt to my regular, systematic Torah study. As the children came, first a girl, then a boy, the urgent financial demands upon me increased, and survival became my prime concern.

The long hours of pressured work took their toll on me and I contracted asthma. I hung on as long as I could, but the harsh winters in New York soon proved too much for me. Finally my cousin, who was also our family doctor, pushed me out of the nest. "For your health's sake...for your family's sake," he told me, "you've got to get out of this climate. You must live in a dryer, more temperate climate. You've got to leave New York and go to Arizona or California."

I knew he was right, so I settled business matters and moved my wife, my two children, and myself to Burbank, California. There I again went into the fur business.

Although I was still neglecting my personal study of Torah, I was determined not to neglect my children's religious training. At that time there were no Orthodox synagogues in Burbank, but one Conservative synagogue had opened only a year before our arrival. This synagogue also had a Hebrew school where we could take our children. So we took them there and began attending ourselves. Our son and daughter were confirmed there and received their bar and bat mitzvahs respectively.

At this synagogue I met Rabbi Joseph Wagner of blessed memory, a real saint. We became good friends, and to our mutual surprise, learned that we had both attended the Yeshivah Rabbenu Yaacov Yoseph in New York City, though at different times. Rabbi Wagner loved Torah. He breathed Torah. When he taught Torah, it became alive to all who heard him. I soon grew to love Rabbi Wagner, and by his godly life and manner he inspired me to "return to Torah" and to again follow its direction for my life.

After a time, Rabbi Wagner moved to another synagogue. The rabbi who followed him was not quite the same, but he also was a Torah-loving rabbi and faithfully taught Torah as Rabbi Wagner had done.

In the course of time, this second rabbi also moved,

and in his place we received a Conservative rabbi, a disciple of Mordecai Kaplan, the founder of the Reconstructionist movement. This movement advocated creative adjustments to contemporary conditions by cultivating traditions and folkways shared by all Jews. Under this man we didn't study Torah. We studied Kaplan's theology, his new civilization. I was saddened, then angered. I was a biblical Orthodox Jew and I hungered for Torah, God's Word. What was I to do?

We attended this synagogue for about two years. During that time I was elected the head of the Education Department. I was happy about that, because I believed that I could insure that our children became well-versed in Torah. At least that is what I thought. But I soon learned that it was an idealistic idea, unfounded on the facts.

When I inspected the school, I was appalled. Apparently nobody knew what was going on. We had engaged a superintendent and paid him an excellent salary. This, both the parents and board thought, should have resulted in a good or even superior school. But this was simply not the case.

The school was hardly better than a glorified babysitting operation. It had no curriculum and nothing with which to study. Our children, our Jewish hope, with their excellent minds, were being destroyed. They were not learning Torah or even Hebrew. They knew nothing of our history, our culture, or our traditions. Nothing Jewish or biblical was being taught.

Our children were almost as ignorant of Jewish things as the *goyim*, the Gentiles. I quickly realized that our young people were being raised in an educational vacuum, and that it would take them four or five years to prepare for their bar or bat mitzvahs.

I was reminded of the charge made by the well-known Orthodox *Rebbetzin* Esther Jungreis when she spoke in Los Angeles. "If our teachers do not teach our children to be Jewish, if they do not teach them God's Word, the Torah, then they are murdering the souls of our youth!"

I heartily agreed with this godly woman, the wife of an Orthodox rabbi. And now, viewing my charge, my sacred trust—our children—the truth of her words hit me with force. If we failed to raise our children to be Jews, soon there would be no Jews, and God's covenant with them would cease to exist. And I, as the one in charge of the school, was now responsible.

I reported my findings to the president. He

shrugged. "What can you do? They're only children."

I remember studying Torah when I was only four, and reminded him of our responsibility. He shrugged again. I reported to the rabbi, with similar results. I took my report to the educational committee. They didn't believe me.

"Our children are not being taught Torah," I said. "They must be taught Torah if they're to prepare for their bar and bat mitzvahs...if they are to prepare for life...."

"Teach them to memorize it," the rabbi said.

"No," I said. "They should know what they are reading. They must learn to read Hebrew, so that they can read from the Torah."

His answer astounded me. "No. Only over my dead body will these children study from the Torah!"

I appealed to the children. Their answers reflected those of their elders. "We don't care about all that," they said. "All we care about is the bar mitzvah party...the presents."

I could no longer tolerate this apathy, this disregard for Torah and biblical Judaism. In order to keep my own integrity, I removed our family from that synagogue and moved it to the newly organized Emunah Orthodox Synagogue in Burbank. At that time the membership was very small, hardly a *minyan,* the minimum number of ten Jews above the age of thirteen required for congregational worship, public Torah reading, and recitation of certain prescribed prayers. But shortly after I came, Dr. Bau arrived with his brother-in-law and two other families. This provided us with a strong *minyan* every Sabbath.

The congregation learned of my interest in preparing young people for their bar and bat mitzvahs, so they made me responsible for their training. I accepted the opportunity with gusto.

The year was 1950, and by then the Jewish State had been established and interest in Zionism was flourishing. Personally, I had always been fascinated with prophecies about biblical Zionism and had occasionally thought I would like to study it.

One day Dr. Bau approached me with an interesting question. "Isidor, I understand you are quite interested in Zionism?"

"Very much so."

"Well, I have been reading of a synagogue that appointed one of their men as Rabbi of Zionism. And I think we should have one in our synagogue."

I agreed.

"Will you become our Rabbi of Zionism?"

"Gladly."

Though I was vitally interested in the subject, I informed Dr. Bau that I was primarily interested in seeing that our children should be exposed to and understand the prophetic teachings as they came up. "The visions of the prophets are beautiful," I told him, "I would like for our children to learn to appreciate and understand them."

Shortly after that conversation, I appeared before the board and was given the official position of Rabbi of Zionism. The declared purpose of this appointment was to research the Scriptures concerning Zionism and then to make my findings known to the congregation.

I lost no time plunging into the subject.

CHAPTER FOUR
TORAH STUDY PRINCIPLES

From the time I was a very small child, I have never had the slightest doubt that Yehovah exists and that I knew him. Nor have I ever doubted that Yehovah is always present, always near. His awesome power is a matter of fact; it has never been debatable. I have always known that he knows me intimately—my inmost thoughts, dreams, aspirations, shortcomings, failures, and sins. Nothing has ever shaken my confidence in him. Without hesitation I can say as Job said, "For I *know* that my Redeemer liveth."

From the day I first learned to pray at my father's knee, I have had instilled in me the firm assurance that Torah, Yehovah's Word, is from everlasting to everlasting. Yehovah's dialogues with Abraham, Isaac, and Jacob are more familiar to me than any secular literature. As a child, the names of

Moses, our Teacher, the Prophets, and scores of other Bible characters were as familiar to me as the names of my family. In fact, these biblical personages were and are my family.

The words they spoke are indelibly engraved upon my mind. With no effort I recall Yehovah's conversation with Moses in the desert, David's praises to the Lord, and the Prophets' exhortations. I never made a conscious effort to memorize the words of the Torah. But simply by continuous association with them, they became an integral part of me, and I knew them. I knew their content, their Author.

Yehovah has always been as close to me as breathing, for he is the Breath of Life. And he has breathed his own life into me. The Presence, his Presence, the *shekinah*...all that Yehovah is, including his *Ruach Hakodesh*, his Holy Spirit, has surrounded me, filled me, guided me, sustained me...even from my earliest recollections.

What is true of my relationship with Yehovah is true of every sincere Jew who lives according to Torah with integrity. When people realize the deep love and loyalty that observant Jewish people have for Yehovah, they will be able to understand just how important it is for us to study Torah.

We believe that every word of Torah is true. We believe that God is exactly who he said he is. We believe that God is to His people everything he said he would be and that he will do exactly what he promised to do.

God spoke to Moses from the burning bush saying, "I have surely seen the affliction of my people...I know their pains...and I am come down to deliver them out of the hands of the Egyptians, and to bring them... unto a land flowing with milk and honey."

Then God told Moses, "I will send thee unto Pharaoh, that thou mayest bring forth my people."

When Moses asked God the name he should use in describing their Deliverer, "God said unto Moses: *Ehyeh asher ehyeh*, I AM THAT I AM'; and he said, 'Thus shalt thou say unto the children of Israel: I AM hath sent me unto you...The Lord, the God of your fathers, the God of Abraham, the God of Isaac, and the God of Jacob, hath sent me unto you; this is My name forever, and this is My memorial unto all generations'" (Exodus 3:7-15).

"Ehyeh asher ehyeh," "I AM THAT I AM." This is the Yehovah I have known since childhood. The One who told Moses, "This is My name forever...(a) memorial unto all generations."

This mighty One who "with His mighty arm" brought His people out of slavery, and who decreed that all peoples should be free—he is the One I have always known. He is the One my father taught me to know, the One who promised to bring deliverance and healing to his People, the One to whom David wrote and sang his psalms of praise, the One of whom the Prophets spoke.

So when my early *yeshivah* teachers said to me, "Only Torah is our textbook," I took their words to mean that *only Torah* in its totality could properly instruct me in the words and ways of this Almighty personage we refer to as Yehovah.

No wonder we were taught that each word of each sentence of Torah was important and was to be studied! No wonder it was so important for each person in *yeshivah* to expound the meaning of each sentence and word (and in some cases, even each letter of each word) of the section under discussion!

In our *bet hamidrash,* or house of research, we were taught definite study principles, principles which have stood me in good stead across my entire lifetime. I applied these principles in preparing young boys and girls for their bar and bat mitzvahs, and I applied them as I began my in-depth *doresh* or research of Zionism in Scripture.

The first of these principles taught us respect for another's point of view. Even if the teacher or a student disagreed with another's viewpoint or opinion, he must show respect, both for that opinion and for the proponent of that opinion. This is not always easy to do.

In the motion picture *Yentl,* more than one *yeshivah* scene depicted the students in loud, demonstrative, seemingly argumentative discussions with each other. These students were not shouting one another down. They were merely loudly proclaiming their individual points of view. When one student was satisfied that the others understood his point of view—whether or not they agreed with it—then he was satisfied. In other words it is not necessarily agreement that is sought, but understanding.

A second *bet hamidrash* principle I frequently espouse (I can still hear it ringing in my ears) is: "If several of you disagree on a matter of exegesis or biblical interpretation, we will record them all. Then every student will investigate *each one of them.* After you have done so, then every one of you is to select the one that best fits your own need, and take it as your own."

One can quickly see the value of this principle.

Left alone, most of us tended to settle comfortably on an interpretation of a Scripture without having personally researched it, simply because our favorite teacher expounded upon this interpretation. But when our minds were expanded as we carefully examined several facets of that Scripture or concept, and then chose the one that seemed right to us, we were more likely to build for ourselves a strong and stable biblical foundation.

A final *bet hamidrash* principle states that "Whenever two major views seem to contradict each other, you must temporarily set them aside, and hope that a third view will eventually be found that will harmonize the two."

I was always taught that it is better for two or more to study the Torah together, and better to do so vocally than silently. In so doing, each student acts as a catalyst for the other. Each stimulates the other or others to greater and deeper insights.

When teaching or being taught by another, Moses warned us to *"Lo sakir paunim,"* "do not recognize the face" (Deuteronomy 1:17). The King James translation reads, "Ye shall not respect persons in judgement; but ye shall hear the small as well as the great; ye shall not be afraid of the face of man; for the judgment is God's."

In other words, whether truth comes from a male or female, Jew or Gentile, black or white, or even from the mouth of babes we are to accept it (see Psalm 8:2, or 8:3 in some Bibles).

All of these principles have for their basis the Hebrew key word, *doresh*, "to study, to research." As a young child I learned that once this concept became firmly fixed in my mind, I was then readily able to recognize and obey the scriptural commands that applied to my life.

I have since learned that this same principle applies to any sincere student of the Bible. By learning the importance of God's *words* that are recorded within *God's Word*, then learning the principle of unquestioning obedience, every child of God will be able to live a life of peace, power, and daily victory.

These are unequivocal biblical principles: research (*doresh*) with integrity equals knowledge and insight. Knowledge and insight, plus obedience, equals God's rich rewards. When I learn to *know* what God is saying to me in his Word, I must obey what he says. Then he is honor-bound to answer the promises in his Word.

So, once a student dedicated himself to the twin virtues of research and obedience, he soon learned to recognize God's scriptural commands as he read them. A few of these I have translated literally from the Hebrew:

"Research (*doresh*) Yehovah and his strength; seek his face eternally" (1 Chronicles 16:11). If I am to entrust myself to God, I must be aware of what it means. And if I learn for myself of his strength, his power, his might, then I can confidently relax in his care.

"Research (*doresh*) Yehovah if you are to find him. Call upon him, for he is always near" (Isaiah 55:6). How wonderful to know that he is available, and that when we seek (research) for him in his Word, that we will find him, "for he is always near."

"Those who know thy name will trust thee, for thou hast not forsaken them who research (*doresh*) thee, Yehovah" (Psalm 9:11). How does one come to know his name? By study, by research.

"I researched (*doresh*) Yehovah and he answered me, and from all my confusions he saved me" (Psalm 34:5). What a promise! When I sought him through his Word, he readily responded to my urgent needs! *Baruch ha Shem!* Praise his Name!

"Those who research (*doresh*) Yehovah will never lack the goodness of life" (Psalm 34:11). How can anyone say that our great God is not interested in the most intimate details of our lives? Or that he is not concerned about such "mundane" things as our food, clothing, and shelter?

"When the meek saw they became glad. Those who will research (*doresh*) Yehovah, their (dead) hearts will be made alive" (Psalm 69:33). Again, in addition to our physical well-being, God is interested in our emotional well-being. He wants us to be glad, happy and vibrant with his joy and his peace. All this and more he promises to all his children, when we seek, research, study and *know* him through his Word.

I never cease to be amazed as I look at these references and the scores of others like them. God evidently expects us to seek him with all of our powers. When we do, we have his Word that we will "find" him and "know" him. Of course, the connotation in this finding and knowing is that we will then offer ourselves to him in total obedience.

Great rewards are to be had by obeying the words of God. For example, Deuteronomy 28:13: "If you will listen to the commandments of Yehovah your God which I command you to listen and obey, then you shall be the *head* and not the *tail*."

This same terminology is often used by other prophets. The meaning is clear. If we listen to and obey God's words, we will not be as a "tail" wagging in agreement with the pagans and unbelieving, nonreligious Jews or Christians. It means that if we listen to and obey God's Word we will be wise and will be rewarded for our wisdom. We will not be afflicted by "the spirit of stupidity" (Isaiah 29:9).

English renderings of this verse do not do full justice to the literal Hebrew meaning, which is quite full and expressive. In context, the Prophet spoke of those who fought against Zion, or who refused to heed and obey his Word. The King James Version reads, "Stay yourselves and wonder; cry ye out, and cry...." However, the Hebrew rendering is "Stupefy yourselves, and be stupid! Blind yourselves and be blind!" In other words, those who hear God's words, who understand his desire for their obedience, but who refuse to obey him, are the ones who are acting stupidly and afflicting themselves with blindness. This I have determined not to do.

וַיֵּצֵא חֹטֶר מִגֶּזַע יִשָׁי וְנֵצֶר מִשָּׁרָשָׁיו יִפְרֶה

MY SEARCH

Once, while I was taking a class at a Jewish educational institution, the question was raised concerning the Messianic prophecies. The professor responded, "Do not attempt to study any of these prophecies concerning the coming of the Messiah on your own. It's too dangerous. Don't study them unless you do so with a rabbi who is able to interpret them for you."

"Are any classes ever offered on the subject?" I asked. He smiled benignly at me. "Of course not."

The professor's obviously protective attitude intrigued me. I began to wonder if he and the other teaching rabbis were trying to hide something from the rest of us. Since I received no satisfaction from that professor, I went to another Jewish institution and inquired, "Do you offer any classes on the coming of the Messiah?"

The answer was a flat, "No."

"Are any planned in the future?" I asked.

Again the answer was negative. "No classes are presently being conducted on Messiah's coming...nor are any such classes being contemplated."

All of this seemed strange to me. The coming of the Messiah is anticipated at every Jewish Passover *Seder.* We sing and read of the Messiah during each Sabbath and High Holy Day celebration. And the Messiah's coming is a looked-forward-to event in the heart of every Jew. Still our educational institutions were silent on the subject. I didn't understand.

The non-answers I received intrigued, frustrated, and angered me. Being the "rebel" that I am, I determined that one day I would do something about that apparent vacuum in our Jewish studies.

Now that I was Zionist Rabbi for our synagogue, despite the fact that I was finding Biblical Zionism referred to in more Scriptures than any other facet of Judaism, I again realized that I was facing a vacuum. Furthermore, to my astonishment, I found that practically every prophecy in which the word Zion was used was in some way connected with the Messiah.

For example, I read, "For the sake of Zion" that our Lord "would not be quiet," and "the Redeemer will come to the Zionists," and scores of other such references. Again, as I had before, I wondered why I had never heard these passages discussed publicly.

Since satisfactory answers were not immediately forthcoming, I found myself with two choices: I could either forget the whole matter or I could seek out answers for myself. I decided on the latter.

I knew that the *goyim*, the Gentiles, accepted the Messiahship of *Yeshuah*, whom they called Jesus, by faith, which was beyond my comprehension. Of course, I had heard about this Jesus, but I knew little about him. I knew that he was a Jew and that he was a rabbi. I, as any Jew, could easily accept those facts concerning him. But, according to the rumors I had heard about this Jesus, he had been crucified because he had claimed to be one with Yehovah. In other words, he claimed to be God. I took little stock in the claims Jesus had reportedly made of himself, including his filial relationship with Yehovah.

As far as I was concerned, all that was beside the point and had nothing whatever to do with my present research. It didn't even enter into my mind that I might be researching anything to do with this Jesus.

All I knew was that, as a Jew, "faith" had little to do with the acceptance of any belief. It was objective research that mattered. All of my training demanded that I research the Scriptures to find answers. Only when my mind had been convinced of a truth was I to believe and accept it. This is what I had been trained to do and what I had always done.

Only incidentally did this Jesus enter the picture at all. I was researching Zionism. If the study of Zionism were to somehow point to asking questions about the Gentiles' Messiah, well and good. But if not, that was also good. I was like a scientist, searching for truth wherever it might lead. If somewhere along the way the road signs were to direct me to attempt to prove or disprove *Yeshuah's* claim to Messiahship, then I would do so. If I did, I assured myself that I would throw the entire weight of my training into the task.

At any rate, having little certainty as to where my project would take me, I felt a certain excitement as I set out. I believed that I could be relatively objective. No Christian had ever discussed the subject of Jesus with me. No Christian had ever presented me with his views, nor attempted to "convert" me to his church or to his belief. I was not sick or terminally ill. Nor was

I faced with some catastrophic tragedy. I was well and in my right mind. No emotional motive or need impelled me.

I was well aware that no Orthodox rabbi would deny that there is to be a Messiah and a Messianic Age of Zionism. As Zionist Rabbi, my responsibility was to check every single prophecy that had to do with the coming Messiah. Each jot and tittle would have to be examined for one hundred percent accuracy. Nothing less would suffice. I, Rabbi Isidor Zwirn, would conduct my study with integrity. I would take the prophecies one at a time, research each one thoroughly, then summarize my conclusions.

I knew that this would be the only way I could come to know *Adonai,* who is also called "My Son" (Psalm 2:7), "the Son of God" (Daniel 3:25), and "the Son of man" (Daniel 7:13).

Early in my research I realized that this Divine Person I was researching could be and probably was the same child to which Isaiah referred when he prophesied, "For a child shall be born, a son has been given" (Isaiah 9:6). While I was pondering that verse, I wondered if the powerful king described by Isaiah in the latter part of that same verse might be the one upon whose shoulders the government would be, and whose name would "be called Wonderful Counselor to the Strong God, the Everlasting Father, the Prince (or Ruler) of Peace." I asked myself, might not both of these descriptions apply to the same person?

These possibilities piqued my already aroused curiosity and spurred me on. And I, hardly daring to imagine what my research might uncover, threw myself into the quest with abandon.

This was not a simple task. Over forty major prophecies and numerous other minor ones needed to be investigated. Each of them had to be listed, categorized, and meticulously examined—each context, each word, each letter. I knew it was an extensive task. Yet I had always been taught that eternal truths do not fear the light of intense scrutiny. Since I was determined to know the truth, I opened my Torah and my lexicon and went to work.

Like a scientist, I began by making notes of my findings. Soon my one notebook became two, then three, stuffed with my findings. I was still involved with my synagogue duties, so I was unable to carry on this research full time. But each day I would complete my other obligations, then hurry back to my research.

Throughout the entire course of my research, it seemed that the Lord Adonai was telling me, "Don't hurry. Take your time. Do a good job. Put my light on top of the bushel so you can see well...and so others can also benefit from the results of your investigations."

As I began listing all the Zionist references, I was surprised that there were so many. I also discovered that each major "tap root" prophecy branched off into innumerable smaller but no less important roots. I listed these as well and eventually followed each one to its source.

What I had initially thought would be a rather straightforward undertaking was growing more complex and intricate by the day. Still, with the distinct sense of being led by the *Ruach Hakodesh*, the Spirit of Truth, I continued my lists, and devised an orderly method for dissecting and examining each entity, no matter how major or minor it might appear.

For months I systematically examined each of the prophecies. I checked and rechecked, then carefully tabulated each new piece of information that came to light. My notebooks began to bulge with facts, and my mind began to stagger with new possibilities. Throughout this intensive investigation process, I was filled with living energy unlike anything I had ever known. Each day as I opened my Bible I was freshly struck with a euphoric sense of adventure and discovery.

It was almost as though I were the first person ever to see and comprehend the exciting truths that were becoming mine with each passing hour.

I knew that God had provided us with a twofold test by which to check the veracity of a prophet's words. If a prophet's work passed this two-pronged test, he was considered to be a true and faithful prophet. Conversely, if his work did not stand up to this scrutiny, he was clearly not a prophet, but was some sort of charlatan.

First, did this person's prophetic utterances come to pass? Second, would his words stand the test of time? Would they be studied? Would they apply to another century as they applied at the time they were first uttered?

I applied these two tests to each of the prophecies dealing with Zionism and the Jews' Messiah. Then, one by one, I sorted and selected the ones that passed.

It would take a very large book to detail my total investigation of the Zionist Scriptures and to give an exposition of each of the prophecies I researched. If I were to provide a running account or demonstration of the details involved in this research, one could understand why it took me as long as it did.

Logically, I chose Isaiah as the first and possibly

the primary book of the Bible for my investigation. Isaiah was given the honor of being placed first in the section we call "The Prophets." This was done for a number of reasons, one being that he was probably the most logical and chronological in his presentation of the message Yehovah gave him to convey.

In the first chapter I saw something that immediately caught my eye. In the first few verses, the Prophet is speaking of the rebellion of God's children. This was familiar territory to me. I knew that God had chosen the Jewish people to be a light to the Gentiles (Isaiah 42:6), but that they became rebellious and strayed away from his leading.

What I had not seen before was that when they rebelled, *they did not rebel against Yehovah.* Instead, they rebelled against "the Holy One (literally, the *Holiest One)* of Israel" (v. 4), which I realized was the Messiah! In his opening statements of his first chapter, *the Prophet Isaiah was speaking about the Messiah.*

CHAPTER SIX
THE PLOT THICKENS

Why hadn't I noticed this before? I couldn't say. Though I had read and reread the Prophet Isaiah many times, it seemed that this day I was reading these words with new eyes. I was seeing what I hadn't seen before in words that had been there all along.

"Ah, sinful nation," God was saying through the Prophet, "a people laden with iniquity, a seed of evildoers, children that deal corruptly; they have forsaken the Lord, they have condemned *the Holy One of Israel*." Because Israel rebelled against this Holiest One of Israel, the Messiah, she would "turn away backward," that is, back to the wilderness from which Moses had extricated them.

The final result, the Prophet said, would be disaster. Verses 5 through 7 describe that downward progression until finally, the fate of Israel, "the daughter of Zion," would be that of an empty booth in a vineyard, or like a lodge in a garden of cucumbers, both pictures of temporary shelters for the gardeners, or "as a besieged city." Israel's forthcoming rebellion against the Messiah would result in total desolation!

Isaiah recorded Yehovah's plea for Israel to reconsider her downward ways, to "come now, and let us reason together." If they would do this, Isaiah said, Yehovah promised forgiveness and restoration, and he would cause them to "eat the good of the land" (v. 19). But refusal would cause Israel to "be devoured with the sword." "For the mouth of the Lord hath spoken."

I became alarmed at what I was reading, truly comprehending it for the first time. Was it possible that the terrible persecutions, the pogroms, the ghettos, the destructions, and even the Holocaust of World War II had come upon the Jewish people across the centuries of their own doing?

Was it possible that they had simply been reaping the results of rebellion against "the Holiest One of Israel," against the Messiah? It was a chilling thought.

I couldn't stop here. I had to go on. I carefully read all of Isaiah in Hebrew. I read it again and again. As I did, the picture began coming clear to me. Why hadn't I seen it before?

In the first half of chapter 2 the Prophet delineated

the blessings and rewards that would come to Israel if they would return to Yehovah, walk in his ways and follow his directives. "And it shall come to pass in the end of days (when Israel ceases her rebellion), that the mountain of the Lord's house shall be established as the top of the mountains, and shall be exalted above the hills; and all nations shall flow into it" (v. 2). This, I realized, was to be Israel's destiny.

In Jewish thought this is to be the *Olam Haba*, the world to come, when peace shall be every man's portion, and Messiah shall reign, when there shall be both a new heaven and a new earth.

This will be the glorious day when "many peoples shall go and say: 'Come ye, let us go up to the mountain of the Lord, to the house of the God of Jacob; and he will teach us his ways, and we will walk in his paths.' For out of Zion shall go forth the law, and the word of the Lord from Jerusalem."

When this happens, the Prophet said, the people "shall beat their swords into plowshares, and their spears into pruning hooks. Nation shall not lift up sword against nation, neither shall they learn war any more."

Those were the blessings, the rewards that would come to Israel, if she were to respond to Yehovah's plea to "come and reason together." But from about mid-point of chapter 2 through chapter 6 the Prophet spelled out the horrible results, the punishments that would come if Israel refused to be the light of the world and to establish peace upon the earth.

With deepening awareness, I was beginning to see that if we Jews had heeded the warnings of Moses and of all the other prophets, and if we had returned to Yehovah and walked in his ways as he had repeatedly begged us to do, all the destructions that have come upon us could have been averted. As it was, our refusal to obey him resulted in the repeated sufferings and holocausts.

At this point in my study, being already quite familiar with the fate of the Ten Northern Tribes of Israel, I turned my attention to chapter 7. But I did so with considerable curiosity and apprehension. With the blueprint of Israel's approaching doom spread before me, I asked myself, "Is it fair? Were the Ten Northern Tribes given adequate warning of the impending calamity that would befall them?"

I soon had my questions answered. The first verse set the stage for a very dramatic scene: "And it came to pass in the days of Ahaz the son of Jotham, the son of Uzziah, king of Judah, that Rezin the king of Aram (or

Syria), and Pekah the son of Remaliah, king of Israel, went up to Jerusalem to war against it; but could not prevail against it (or, could not take it)."

This was a very serious situation: King Pekah of Ephraim (the Ten Northern Tribes) had formed an alliance with King Rezin of Syria, who had one of the mightiest armies in the world at that time. Their combined armies went up against Jerusalem to take it. This rebellion of the Ten Tribes against the house of David (or Judah)—Jew against Jew—was the greatest disaster in the history of Judah, an act that resulted in the gravest of consequences.

But neither Ephraim (the Ten Northern Tribes) nor Syria took into account the fact that God was watching over Judah, over Jerusalem. Even though the hearts of the Jerusalemites "moved...as the trees of the forest are moved with the wind" (in fear), the combined forces of Syria and Ephraim were unable to prevail against Jerusalem, the City of God. The reason, of course, was God's divine protection.

Now, for the question that was beginning to plague me: Had Israel (also called the Northern Tribes, the Ten Tribes, or Ephraim) been given adequate warning to cease and desist from their alliance with Syria and to turn from their wicked ways lest tragedy come upon them? I had to know the answer. Because if Israel *had* been properly and adequately warned, any resultant tragedy would be their own responsibility.

I read on. The Lord spoke to Isaiah and told him to go to King Ahaz and tell him, "Thus saith the Lord...." He said that nothing would come of King Pekah's alliance with Syria, except evil for King Pekah and Ephraim, and that "within threescore and five years shall Ephraim be broken, that *it shall not be a people*" (v. 8). Furthermore, he said that God would treat both Syria and Ephraim as one country ruled by two kings (v. 16) and the "two kings thou hast a horror of shall be forgotten."

But King Ahaz refused to believe that Isaiah's words came from the Lord. Isaiah told him, "Ask thee a sign of the Lord (concerning the truth of my words)" (v. 11).

"But Ahaz said: 'I will not ask, neither will I try the Lord'" (v. 12).

Although King Ahaz of Judah refused to believe Isaiah, and refused to ask a sign from God (that is, he refused to believe that Isaiah's prophecies were from the Lord, and to act upon them), God nevertheless promised that an "Emmanuel" (God with us) would come who would be on hand to witness the horrors that were to befall Ephraim and Syria: to wit, that those two kings and their peoples would fall beneath the combined weight of the armies of Assyria and Egypt (vv. 18-20). When that time came, all the land would "become briers and thorns" (v. 24). In other words, desolate.

The plot was thickening. I was beginning to see a definite pattern emerging. God *had* warned his people. He *had* told them disaster would come if they refused to obey his commands. And he *had* promised that one day an "Emmanuel" would come to them. In other words, he had promised that the time was coming when he would be *with* them in the flesh, that he would be with them in Person.

In Chapter 8 of Isaiah, God repeated his warning that Assyria would destroy both Ephraim and Syria. At this point, everything I read augured nothing but doom and gloom for the Ten Northern Tribes. Had they no ray of light, no hope?

CHAPTER SEVEN
A GREAT LIGHT FORETOLD

I turned to Chapter 10 of Isaiah, which I had read scores of times before, and read it again. As I did so, it seemed that my question was being answered: Hope *was* promised; a Deliverer *would* come. But was this deliverer to be the Messiah, the one Christians call Jesus? Had he already come? I needed to find the answer to these questions, too.

Verse 1 of Chapter 10 in my Hebrew Bible begins, "The people that walked in darkness *have seen* a great light...." This, I realized, was not speaking of the past, but of the future. In other words, "the people that walked in darkness would see (at some future date) a great light."

Reading on, slowly and carefully, I had the feeling that I was on the verge of a tremendous discovery. The rest of verse 1, through verses 3 and 4 (vv. 4 and 5 in some Bibles), spoke of the joy that would result from the coming of that great light. It spoke of the "yoke," the "staff," and the "rod" of the oppressors, and how those symbols of bondage and slavery were to be broken.

How could this happen? Who or what would bring this to pass? I caught my breath as I read the answer: "A Child shall be born unto us, a Son has been assigned to us, and the government shall be upon his shoulder. And they shall call his name...."

I read those last eight Hebrew words letter by letter: *Pele joez el gibbor abi ad sar shalom,* then translated them in English. "And they shall call his name *a wonderful Counselor to the Almighty God and Everlasting Father, (also) Prince of Peace."* This could be no other than the Messiah! Because certainly no finite being could counsel the Almighty God.

But, I wondered, what was the purpose of all this? Why would the Messiah counsel Almighty God? Verse 6 gave me the answer (v. 7 in some Bibles): "That the government may be increased (or strengthened), and of peace there shall be no end, upon the throne of David, and upon his kingdom, to establish it, and to uphold it through justice and through righteousness from henceforth and even for ever."

I realized that I was reading a description of the

Messianic Age, the age when Messiah would reign.

With great sadness I read the remainder of the chapter. I could see that the Prophet spoke these anguished words as though they were being wrung from the heart of God himself. Despite Yehovah's warnings, despite his pleadings, despite the offer of his great love to his wayward people, they would not hear him. They would not respond to his love.

The result would be tragedy, pain, destruction, famine—all of which the people were to bring upon themselves. Even so, God promised them his love—"His hand is stretched out still" (v. 20, v. 21 in some Bibles).

What would be the end result of all this? Chapter 10 spelled it out in detail. Assyria, the mightiest army of the then known world, would be the tool used to bring about the demise and destruction of the Ten Northern Tribes. For her part in this, Assyria would be punished, along with the Ten Northern Tribes.

Would any in Israel (or Ephraim) escape this holocaust? Yes, a remnant (vv. 20-21) would escape from their conqueror and eventually return to Israel. But *only a remnant* of Israel, that once numbered as the sands of the sea, will return.

Verses 24-34 indicate the absolute certainty of Assyria's total destruction, when their "burden shall depart from off thy shoulder, and his yoke from off thy neck, and the yoke shall be destroyed...."

Though I could see many things I had not thoroughly seen before, I realized that the Assyrian holocaust had come about because of the refusal of Yehovah's people to obey his commands and to walk after his precepts.

But another question remained. Throughout biblical history, Yehovah promised that all twelve tribes of Israelites would not be totally destroyed. He promised the Patriarchs, the Matriarchs, and the Prophets that they would all remain as one eternal family. How, I wondered, would God accomplish this? How would the remnant return? How would Yehovah's dispersed peoples be reunited, brought together to become one again?

This situation, I realized, was similar to the one in which Moses found his people: enslaved, bound, oppressed, with no apparent hope for the future. Yet, in the midst of that dark hopelessness, Yehovah, by his mighty hand, united his people and led them out of their slavery.

But he did it with a messiah: our prophet-teacher Moses. To accomplish such a monumental task as I saw described in Isaiah, I realized, would require more

than a Moses. It would require the appearance of
the long-promised Messiah. How would Yehovah
accomplish this?

With anticipation I turned to Chapter 11. I saw
my answer in the plainest Hebrew I had ever read.
It was not only the answer to my question, it was the
culmination of the quest of my life: my quest for
the Messiah.

The first seven Hebrew words in Chapter 11 are so
startling, so important, so vital to the truth that I was
now seeing for the first time, that I must define each
one of them for you so that you can see the literal
translation of this verse. Though I knew the definitions of each of these words, I used my Hebrew dictionary to be absolutely certain. I encourage readers
to do the same, to look these words up in any good
Hebrew dictionary or lexicon and verify the accuracy
of my definitions.

Those seven Hebrew words that changed the life
of Orthodox Rabbi Isidor Zwirn are *"V'yattzah choter
migetzah yishi, v'netzer mesharsav yifreh."* Word by
word, the Hebrew lexicon defines them:

V'yattzah—there shall come forth
choter—a green branch or green shoot (descendant)

migetzah—a trunk

yishi—of Jesse

v'netzer—to keep or to preserve (or, one who keeps or preserves), to watch over or to guard (or, one who watches over or guards), or to Christianize (all have the same basic meaning)

mesharsav—from its roots

yifreh—to be fruitful or to bear fruit

The *New American Standard Bible* translates this verse: "Then a shoot will spring from the stem of Jesse, and a branch from his roots will bear fruit."

But allow me to reconstruct this verse from the literal Hebrew of Isaiah. The Prophet first presented a picture of a cut-down tree. Then concerning that cut-down tree, he said, "A green branch or shoot (descendant) shall come forth from the trunk of Jesse, and preservation (the protector of Israel, or Christianity) will come from the roots or the stump of that cut-down tree, that will blossom, bud, and bear fruit."

It suddenly became clear to me: In picturesque language Isaiah was telling his readers about the Messiah! Now I understood what the Prophet was talking about: Jesse, David's father, who symbolized the twelve tribes, stood for the remnant, or the "stump" that was to be left after the Assyrian holocaust. And from that stump, David, a name often used as a euphemism for the *Messiah,* was the green branch or shoot that was to come forth from the remnant of Israel.

Taking this possibility a step further, I saw from the context that this "shoot" or "green branch" that would burst forth from the stump of Jesse would be a divine Personage. This had to be, because verse 2 went on to say about him, "The Spirit of the Father Yehovah shall rest upon him, the spirit of wisdom and understanding, the spirit of counsel and might, the spirit of knowledge and of the fear of the Lord."

The weeks and months had rolled by as I researched, but I was hardly conscious of the passage of time. So eager was I to find answers to my questions and a solution to the mysteries that had plagued me for so long that I often studied and worked late into the night.

One such night I came to a place in my research where it all became crystal clear to me. I had been going over and over chapter 11 of Isaiah when I saw another piece to the jigsaw puzzle. In verses 3 through 9 the Prophet was detailing the ministry of this Person, foretelling that, among other things, he "would judge righteously" and that "he would bring peace...."

This, I knew was the acid test of Messiah: *He would bring peace to his people.*

At that point in my study, nothing could distract me. As I delved into verses 9 and 10, I realized I had struck another rich vein of ore. "And it shall come to pass in that day, that *the root* (descendant) *of Jesse,* that standeth for an ensign of the peoples, unto him shall the nations seek; and his resting-place shall be glorious...."

To interpret, "And when he—that root of Jesse—comes in *that day* (the day of Messiah's appearing), this One who stands for the ensign or emblem of Zionism, unto him shall the nations (all people) go to research Torah. And his resting-place shall become glorious (a place upon which honor would be bestowed). Reading this from the Masoretic text, I could see no other conclusion but that his ensign, this "resting-place," was the Cross on which he was crucified.

Where was all this taking me? I, Isidor Zwirn, was speaking of the Cross—the Cross that had become a symbol of Christianity to the world! But I couldn't stop now. I had to go on.

"And it shall come to pass in that day, that the Lord will set his hand *again the second time* to recover the remnant of his people...." The second time? Did that mean that the Messiah had already come a first time? The text certainly seemed to indicate that possibility.

Question: What would happen when he came the second time?

Answer: He would "recover the remnant of his people"! He would recover them from Assyria, Egypt, Cush (Ethiopia), and "from the islands of the sea." In other words, from all over the world, from wherever his people had been dispersed and scattered. "And he will assemble the dispersed of Israel, and gather together the scattered of Judah from the four corners of the earth"!

There was my answer. Messiah would gather all of his people—the Ten Northern Tribes (the so-called "Lost Tribes") and the two tribes of Judah. Messiah would do all this *when he came the second time.* Historically, I knew that, even prior to World War I, but especially since World War II, the Jewish people had been migrating to what was then called Palestine in great numbers. But since May of 1948 when Israel became a state, hundreds of thousands of Jews had migrated to Israel *from all over the world.*

I realized that the prophesied "total gathering

together" of the Jewish nation was still in the process. Like a flash, the significance of that fact came to me: *It most certainly meant that Messiah had already come for the first time, and that his second appearance was drawing nigh!*

Orthodox Jews have always believed that Messiah would come two times. We frequently read and sing in our prayer books, "May we be worthy to live and witness and inherit the good and the blessings of *the two times* of the coming of the Messiah: to live in the Kingdom come....And he will let us hear from him for *the second time* in the presence of the eyes of the living."

By the time I reached this place in my research, though I was not aware of it, a gradual change had occurred in my thinking. I was no longer even faintly apprehensive of where this research might lead me. In fact, I found myself experiencing an almost reckless sense of adventure, an eager anticipation of each new discovery.

Paradoxically enough, considering my Orthodox background, I was almost breathless with the exciting prospect of "discovering" or "meeting" the Messiah in the pages of Torah and the Prophets.

Even if I had wanted to do so, I knew that I had gone too far to turn back. I found myself feeling somewhat impatient with anything that drew me away from my studies. Like a scientist on the trail of a new virus, a hitherto undiagnosed illness, or an as yet unnamed stellar constellation, I single-mindedly pursued my research.

Having mined the rich ore field of Isaiah, I moved on to the second and third of the three major Zionist Scriptures, Jeremiah 31 and Psalm 110. Each claimed my attention for a different reason.

I won't detail my research into these and other Zionist Scriptures as I did into the Book of Isaiah. But suffice it to say, for months the evidence piled up. To the *goyim* mind, my meticulous attention to detail might have been too much. But you must remember that I had been trained to pay attention to every word, in fact, *every letter* of Torah.

Finally, as does any researcher after truth, whether scientist, logician, or theologian, I reached the point where any more effort would have resulted in diminishing returns. I needed to sift and analyze the facts. I opened my bulging notebooks and carefully examined my notes again. They were well in order. My logic was impeccable. All that remained was for me to compile the results.

I drew a deep breath and reached for my pen.

I wrote: "Every single prophecy that I have researched concerning the coming of Messiah is true, and has come to pass *exactly as predicted* by the prophets of Israel."

I leaned back in my chair and thought of the implications of the statement I had just made. It was as though a great light shone from the pages of Torah into the innermost recesses of my being. "The people who sat in darkness...," I thought, Isidor Zwirn among them, "...have seen a great light...." That light was now shining so brightly that I could not deny it. "Thy Word is a lamp unto my feet," came quickly to mind, "and a light unto my path."

Indeed, this must be the light that lights every man who comes into the world. That light was shining upon the pages of my notebook. That light was now focused, a luminous circle of brilliance upon the eternal facts of the case.

Now that the facts were in and the conclusion drawn, what was I, Orthodox Rabbi Isidor Zwirn, to do? I did not cogitate long upon that question. I did as every honest seeker after truth had done when the truth he has sought is finally revealed. I accepted it.

I recognized and acknowledged the simple, yet (for me) earth-shattering fact that the Messiah I so long had awaited *had already come.* He had come to earth nearly 2,000 years ago. He had come "unto his own, and his own had received him not." And the name of that divine Person whom I had so painstakingly sought and found in the pages of Torah was he, *Yeshuah ha Meshiach,* Jesus Christ the Messiah: the Messiah of all mankind, *including the Jews!* Including Rabbi Isidor Zwirn.

The moment I accepted the veracity of that statement, I became, as had the Apostle Paul on the road to Damascus, a follower of that Messiah. I did not know how greatly the acceptance of that plain, well-documented fact would affect my life. Had I really thought about it, I should have known. But I did not hesitate or ponder the consequences of my response to what had become to me the irrevocable, plain truth of Scripture.

So it was, in that wondrously beautiful moment of mental awareness and intellectual commitment, when for the very first time, I not only knew the identity of the Messiah, but in the truest sense of the word, *I knew him!*

So excited was I in that grand moment of discovery, that I did not foresee the immediate and drastic consequences that would result from my decision.

CHAPTER EIGHT
MESHUMMAD!

During the many months of my Zionist
research, I had kept pretty much to myself, except
for my synagogue duties and family responsibilities.
According to Torah, every Jew is responsible to
develop a personal relationship with God, that is, to
know him. His commands to know him are not to be
taken lightly. They are not options that one can
choose to obey or to ignore.

The Lord had commanded me to research
Zionism, so I did my best to obey. Since this was a
personal assignment, I felt no need or desire to share
the results of my ongoing research with anyone,
not even with my wife. My quest had nothing to do
with her nor with my children, nor with the
head rabbi of our synagogue.

Because I was responding to and obeying a commandment God had given me, just as everyone must

attempt to understand and obey God's commandments to them, it seemed perfectly natural and logical
for me to proceed as I did.

I had no more right to impose my search upon
others than they would have had a right to impose
their personal research upon me. I followed God's
directives to me. If he had given the same assignment
to others, that would be all right with me; and how
they handled it would be between them and the Lord.

I had been so immersed in my research that I gave
little thought to how my family might respond when
I told them what I had been doing and the conclusions I had drawn. But I clearly recall what happened
when I broached the subject to them. I didn't make
a big deal of my announcement, I just told them, "I
have come to the conclusion that the *Yeshuah* of
the Christians is also the Messiah of the Jews...."

Looking back now, I doubt that I could have
said anything that could have shocked them more.
The reaction I received from them was, in each case,
instantaneous. First a long moment of stunned silence,
then the outburst. "You converted to Christianity! You've
become a Christian! You converted!"

"No, I didn't convert...I just said—"

"I heard what you said. You said you're a Christian!"

"No, I didn't say that. Just listen to me—"

"I heard what you said. And you said too much already. You said you'd converted, that you're now a follower of that...of that *Jesus*. That's what you said. And I don't want to hear another word about it."

They didn't just pronounce the word Jesus or *Yeshuah*, they spit it out. I had long ago forgotten the fear and hatred that name had once produced in me. But it all came flooding back. I remembered those times on the Lower East Side of New York City when the *goyim* had taunted me with the words, "Christ killer, Jesus killer! You kikes are all Jesus haters!"

Those words the *goyim* shouted were true. I did hate the name which engendered such persecution and violence to us Jewish kids. I hadn't understood who Jesus was. But I did understand that it was because of that name that I was insulted and spit upon and burned with cigarettes.

As I listened to the incriminations being heaped upon me *by my own family* because of that name, I was at first unbelieving, then shocked, then hurt. "You just don't understand...," I tried to tell them.

But they wouldn't listen. "You're no longer a Jew! You're a Christian. You are *meshummad*, a traitor!"

"No...no...," I said. "I'm not a traitor."

"You *are* a traitor to the Jews. Have you forgotten how the Christian crusaders slaughtered our people by the thousands. And how the inquisitors in Spain killed millions—all in the name of that Jesus you now claim to follow? You are *meshummad*, traitor!"

During the next weeks and months that word was flung at me with such bitterness that it often rang in my ears when I tried to sleep. My own family was calling me *meshummad*, traitor.

The word spread like wildfire: "Isidor Zwirn's a Christian!"

My protests were in vain. "I'm not a Christian. I'm a Jew. I was born a Jew and I'll die a Jew...."

They would rebuff me. "How can you call yourself a Jew when you believe in the Christian Jesus? It doesn't make sense."

Paradoxically, I got the same, though oddly opposite, response from the Christians who heard. They would greet me with, "Praise the Lord, Rabbi. I heard that you're now a Christian. That's wonderful news. Now you can go back and *convert* your own people."

In vain I told them, "No! I'm not a Christian. I'm a Jew. I was born a Jew and I'll die a Jew."

This statement was always met with bewilderment. "But you just said...you just said you're a Christian.

And now you say you're still a Jew. I don't understand."

"Just listen," I would try again, "I didn't say I was a Christian. You said I was a Christian. I merely said that I now believe that Yeshuah is the Messiah."

"But that makes you a Christian," they would say, with total lack of comprehension in what I had just told them.

"No. I'm not a Christian," I would try again. "I'm no more a Christian than Jesus was...or Peter...or Paul. They were all Jews. And I'm a Jew. The only difference is that I believe that Jesus, or *Yeshuah,* is the Messiah, *just like the disciples did. Just like those believers in Jerusalem. And they weren't Christians, but Jewish believers in the Messiah. It was the Gentiles, the goyim, followers of Christ who were known as Christians.* Don't you see that?"

Such statements were usually accepted in stony silence, just as they were received by my family and fellow Jews. My words on the subject were apparently about as incomprehensible as they would have been to a Martian or some other outer space creature. It was as though they could not hear the words I was saying. All they could hear *is what they had been taught all their lives:*

"A Jew is a Jew."

"A Christian is a Christian."

"When a Jew believes in Jesus he becomes a Christian."

"Then he is no longer a Jew."

"There is no middle ground."

According to popular tradition, a Jew is either a Jew or he is a Christian. He cannot be both. *A Jew cannot accept the truth, the reality, the fact that Jesus is the Messiah of all mankind without becoming a Christian.*

The paradox was tragically humorous. Both my Jewish family and friends *and the Christians* believed the same thing. If they were united on nothing else, they were united on this common ground: When a Jew begins believing that Jesus is the Messiah, he is no longer a Jew but a Christian. No Jew can possibly retain his Jewish identity and accept the Messiahship of *Yeshuah ha Meshiach*.

What a spot for anyone to be in! What was I to do? My wife, my children, my sister, and my Jewish friends—all of them thought I was crazy. And there was a time when I even wondered about that myself.

I decided to share my knowledge with the senior rabbi of our synagogue. He listened patiently. He didn't try to dissuade me. All he said was, "Just don't talk about that around here."

I agreed, and thought that might be the end of the matter. But I was mistaken. At that time I was taking some classes at a local university. Everyone there knew I was a Jew, which I had never made any bones about; but now I began talking about something that no Jew should talk about. I began telling my classmates that *Yeshuah* was the Messiah. It caused an uproar on the campus.

The news of this got back to my synagogue by means of a student who was the son of one of the synagogue men. "Rabbi Zwirn is telling everyone on the campus that Jesus is the Messiah!" he reported to his father. His father reported it to the council. It might have gone no further, had not the Los Angeles Orthodox Jewish Council stepped in.

"This is disgraceful," they said. So they did something about it. They sent a communique to the council of my synagogue. "Unless Rabbi Zwirn is physically prevented from participating in synagogue services, we will cease to recognize the orthodoxy of your synagogue."

That did it. The following Sabbath as I stepped up to the *bimah* to participate in the service, two burly policemen appeared, ushered me out of the synagogue, and ordered me to stay out.

וְיֵצֵא חֹטֶר מִגֵּזַע יִשָׁי וְנֵצֶר מִשָּׁרָשָׁיו יִפְרֶה

CHAPTER NINE
AFTER THE FACT

Thinking back, even though I was and will always remain a Jew, I should have anticipated my fellow Jews' reaction. I realize that I was naively unprepared for the explosive reception that resulted from my announcement that I, Orthodox Rabbi Isidor Zwirn, now believed that the feared and hated Jesus of the Christians was actually the Jews' long-awaited Messiah, and that he was indeed, *Yeshuah ha Meshiach,* Jesus the Messiah.

I thought they would be as eager as I to accept the results of my investigation. But they were not. With hardly a single exception, my announcement was met incredulity. And, in practically every case, the incredulity immediately turned into anger, then from anger into hatred—sheer, unadulterated, naked hatred.

It is difficult even for a Jew to understand the hatred directed at another Jew who becomes a *meshummad,* a believer, a traitor. So I know it is utterly impossible for any non-Jew to understand what happens within the Jewish community when a Jew declares that he has become a follower of the Messiah. Often the *meshummad* is declared to be deceased, his funeral is held, and the *Kaddish,* a prayer of mourning, is read for the departed—all exactly as would happen when a death occurred.

Jews are helpless to combat this anger, for our rabbis have built into the Jewish system this impregnable wall of hatred for the past 2,000 years. It is almost a reflex action, an automatic response to what we call the unthinkable. In the Jewish community, from the moment a Jew begins to follow *Yeshuah* (which I now realize is happening with greater regularity), he is considered no longer to be a Jew. For a Jew, the acceptance of the Messiahship of Jesus is a contradiction in terms. All of this is not easy for a non-Jew to comprehend. Perhaps it is just as difficult for a Jew to understand.

Much later I was to learn that Jesus called this unfounded and unjust hatred of Jew for Jew *sinas chinum,* hatred without a cause. He said, "Now have they both seen and hated both me and my Father. But this cometh to pass, that the word might be fulfilled that is written in their law, They hated me without a cause" (John 15:25). Jesus quoted those words from Psalm 69:5 (v. 4 in some versions).

I knew none of this at that time because my knowledge of *Yeshuah ha Meshiach* had come entirely from Torah, and I was almost totally ignorant of the writings contained in the *B'rit Chadeshah*, the New Testament.

That *sinas chinum* Jesus spoke of began with me as it began with him, within the immediate family. Long after my own trauma, I was to learn of the persecution that came to Jesus by his own people when they "went out to take custody of him; for they were saying, 'He has lost his senses'" (Mark 3:21).

The whole Jewish community verified Jesus' prediction. My own family thought I had lost my senses. My wife, my children and my entire family, except for my grandchildren, became enraged when I announced the result of my research. I can't blame them. Had my wife been the first one to declare her belief in *Yeshuah ha Meshiach* I would also have felt betrayed and angry at her.

It was impossible to reason with any of them. When I asked them to "come now and let us reason together" (Isaiah 1:18), they refused. It seemed that their reasoning faculties had been overruled by their hatred.

After a time, though, when I refused to strike back, and when they all saw our Lord's law of love in action in my life, their anger and hatred began to subside.

At the time I was taking classes in Jewish studies at a local college. I thought that surely these Jewish professors might "come and reason together" with me. But I was mistaken. All my attempts to share my new discoveries with my peers, my professors, and even with the Jewish head of the philosophy department met with disappointment. Though I had received an A from him on my midterms, this man failed me on my finals, but was unable to produce my exam paper at the Dean's request. When I decided to retake the class, this professor had the campus police bar my entrance to his classroom.

I was so excited about my new discovery that I shared it with the president of our synagogue. Though he didn't agree with my conclusions, he was charitable toward me. He merely requested that I not speak of my belief in *Yeshuah* in or near the synagogue, which I agreed to do.

But the exciting truths I had unearthed in Torah could not be denied. I shared my light with everyone who would listen. This brought about my sudden removal from the Orthodox synagogue I had been a part of for years.

The persecution didn't stop there. A newly arrived rabbi at the Conservative synagogue attempted to have me ousted from the Burbank Ministerial Association. A committee was appointed and an investigation held, which found me blameless. Grateful for their positive report, I remained a member of the ministerial association for another two years.

It seemed that all doors were closing to me. My family would not listen to me. My professors and fellow students would have nothing to do with me. My longtime friends and synagogue fellowmembers rejected me.

Like Rabbi Paul (the Apostle Paul), it seemed that I had become a nonperson among my family, friends, and associates. Following the moment when sight came to his blinded eyes, that rabbi spent many years in Arabia before he was accepted by his brethren. Was this also to be my lot? I wondered.

As difficult as my situation had become, as with Rabbi Paul, I was soon to face another challenge and weather yet another disappointment, this time from an unexpected quarter.

With all the publicity in the college student publications and the Burbank newspapers, along with the word-of-mouth information about my activities, it was inevitable that I would come to the attention of some Christian churches. It appears that it is a custom among Christians to invite people who have come to *Yeshuah* to give a "testimony" of how it happened. This testimony is usually embellished by an account of some "miraculous event," including details concerning how some friend or other trusted person was instrumental in their "conversion." This custom is especially adhered to when a Jewish person begins to follow *Yeshuah*.

So on numerous occasions I found myself in the rather awkward predicament of being asked to give my "testimony." I say "awkward" because from my point of view, I had no dramatic story to tell. No "miraculous event" had brought me to my "decision" to believe and follow the Messiah. I was not faced with any tragedy or catastrophe in my life that impelled me to seek "salvation." Nor had there been other humans involved in the experience. As a matter of fact, the opposite had been true. No Christian that I knew had ever bothered to discuss my Jewishness with me nor tried to "convert" me. I had come to

Yeshuah completely on my own. My own research had resulted in my eyes becoming opened.

But when I related this story to Christians, they wouldn't believe me. It seems that they would not (or could not) accept the fact that no one had ever "presented Jesus to me." They adamantly insisted that what I had done was wrong, that it was impossible to have come to the knowledge of Jesus as I had. They insisted that it was absolutely necessary to accept Jesus "by faith," which was the "regular formula."

Christians rejected the fact that I had followed the Prophet Isaiah's admonition to "Research (*doresh*) the Lord, for he can be found, research him, for he is near" (Isaiah 55:6; literal translation from the Hebrew). It seemed beyond their comprehension that anyone, especially a Jew, could have become a follower of the Messiah with no one to guide him.

Yet this is the way that religious Jews have always come to the Messiah. From young childhood they have known the Scriptures (as the Apostle Paul said of young Timothy), and by knowing them, have learned to know God. In other words, their faith in the integrity of the Scriptures has brought them to a living, viable relationship with Yehovah, our Father.

The Scriptures say, "Without faith it is impossible

to please him (Yehovah)...." The observant Jew has faith in God, because, from childhood, he has known him.

"For he that cometh to God must believe that he is (that he exists)...." The observant Jew possesses the unshakable assurance that God is (that he exists).

"And that he is the rewarder of them that diligently research (*doresh*) him" (Hebrews 11:6).

As a Jew, a religious Jew, an observant Jew, I had always had faith in Yehovah; I had always known him. And now, as I had researched the Scriptures, the Torah, the Prophets, with integrity, being assisted by the *Ruach haemet* (the Spirit of Truth), my eyes were opened (Luke 24:31), and I recognized *Yeshuah* to be the Messiah. That simple recognition was my acceptance of him.

The Christians who interrogated me didn't know, and seemed uninterested in learning, that many Jews are coming to the Messiah through the Spirit of Truth, just as I had. When I told them that I had come to know or *da'at* Jesus through the prophetic facts in the Old Testament, just as Jesus prophesied, the Christians seemed unable to believe me. And they were not at all interested in discussing the matter with me or in researching the matter for themselves in the writings of Israel's prophets of truth.

The church people of any denomination I had occasion to meet were all courteous and respectful of me. (They treated me as an oddity which they didn't quite know how to categorize.) But they were unanimous in their attempts to "convert" me to their particular church or denomination. When I told them that I intended to remain faithful to the religion that Jesus practiced, they became troubled and apprehensive. They obviously had no frame of reference with which to comprehend my stand.

When I appealed to them to search out and discover their own biblical roots in Abraham and Judaism, my words fell upon deaf ears. I tried to tell the Christians that they were not *goyim* as defined by the Jews, a somewhat derisive term that means "heathen" or "pagan," but they would not hear me and continued to refer to themselves as Gentiles.

In the light of the training I had received and the kind of thinking I had practiced as a child, it was incomprehensible to me that none of these Christians would sit down with me in a *bet hamidrash* manner and study what Torah predicted about *Yeshuah ha Meshiach*, Jesus; the *notzrim*, Christians; and the *B'rit Chadeshah*, the New Testament.

Their reluctance caused me to wonder if they

were running from the responsibility of being the "light of the world" as Jesus had charged them to be. Their attitude seemed to reflect an inferiority complex regarding Jews which meant they were still *goyim:* Gentiles. I wondered if it was because they feared the *Ruach haemet,* the Spirit of Truth, the Helper, which *Yeshuah* taught would testify that Jesus is "the Way, the Truth, and the Light." I visited many Christian churches in the hope that I might encounter at least some understanding or acceptance of my position. But without a single exception, all of these attitudes were expressed by all the Christians I met.

The Hebrew Christian churches were little different. For the most part, they were financed by mainline denominational churches with the declared purpose of "converting" Jews to become *goyisha,* Gentilized Christians. I didn't find a single one that had as its goal the fulfillment of the prophecies that the Jews were to return to the biblical Judaism of the prophets of Israel, and thus become *shalem,* completed Jews.

After stumbling from one Christian church to another for many months, it became appallingly clear to me that precious few Christians had any knowledge of Torah, and thus were unable to allow *Yeshuah* to decide who was to be a part of the eternal

Tree of Life, the Body of Christ.

Therefore none of them fully understood the import of my words when I told them, "I was born a Jew like Jesus, and I'll die a Jew like him." Nor did they seem to understand when I reminded them that if all Jews "converted" and became assimilated that there would soon be no Jews left. And God promised that the Jews would never cease to be. When I made these apparently "heretical" statements they were no longer interested and began to ignore me.

It seemed that gradually I was being excommunicated from and hated by all, exactly as forewarned by Jesus (Matthew 10:22; 24:9; Mark 13:13; Luke 21:12, 16-17), with exactly the same *sinas chinum* (Jew-against-Jew hatred "without a cause") that has been present in the world for the past 2,000 years. When that happened, I had nowhere to go. Neither my own Jewish people nor the Christians would accept me. I was not welcome in synagogues or churches. I didn't fit in either place. I began to identify with Jesus when he said, "The birds have nests and the foxes have holes, but the Son of man has no place to lay his head" (Matthew 8:20).

I also identified with John the Baptist. Like him, I was "a voice crying in the wilderness." I understood

Jesus to declare that "salvation is of the Jews" (John 4:22), and had tried to take my message "to the Jews first." In every way that I knew, I had tried to be a witness "in Jerusalem." Still, it seemed that everywhere I met with failure and rejection.

Nevertheless, it was not all for naught. I did learn that anyone, Jew or Greek (Gentile or Barbarian), can come to know our Lord *Adonai* through the Spirit of Truth. I learned that anyone who researched him with integrity in the same manner in which he researched our Father *Yehovah* and Holy Spirit *Elohim,* the fullness (*echad*) of *the One Living God can be found.*

Our Father guarantees it. "And ye shall seek me, and find me, when ye shall search (*doresh*) for me with all your heart. And I will be found of you, saith Yehovah" (Jeremiah 29:13-14).

CHAPTER TEN
I DISCOVER THE NEW TESTAMENT

Up to this point, I had accepted the *B'rit Chadeshah,* or New Testament, because of what the Prophets had said. After all, they were the ones who had predicted the Gospel, this Good News of Messiah's appearance, an event which I now realized had already come to pass. I had often read Jeremiah's account of this great day. "'Behold, days are coming,' declares the Lord, 'when I will make a new covenant with the house of Israel and with the house of Judah, not like the covenant which I made with their fathers in the day I took them by the hand to bring them out of the land of Egypt, my covenant which they broke, although I was a husband to them,' declares the Lord.

"'But this is the covenant which I will make with the house of Israel after those days,' declares the Lord. 'I will put my law within them, and on their heart I will write it; and I will be their God, and they shall be my people'" (Jeremiah 31:31-33).

And now, as a follower of Messiah, I began re-searching the "New Covenant" of which Jeremiah and the other Prophets wrote, the *B'rit Chadeshah,* the New Testament, with the same intensity that I had applied to my Torah studies.

I realized that this *B'rit Chadeshah* that I now held in my hands was absolute proof of the veracity, the lit-eral fulfillment of the Prophet's words. As the Prophet had said, this was the "New," or perhaps more literally, the "Renewed Covenant." And it contained eternal truths just the same as the Torah.

Yet, each time I began reading the English *B'rit Chadeshah,* I was aware of a strange uneasiness which I could not explain. That strangeness persisted each time I opened it, and I realized that I scarcely under-stood what I was reading. My comprehension of its message was practically nil. The disturbing thought came to me that perhaps only a Christian scholar could derive joy and practical benefit from the study of this Book, and for a time I considered enrolling in a Christian seminary or Bible school.

Then our Lord impressed me to read the *B'rit Chadeshah* in Hebrew. As I did so, an interesting thing happened. This previously "strange" Book with its "strange" culture and tongue became as clear and logical as Torah. Its pages came alive and took on the glow of the Prophets of Israel.

For the first time I began receiving the kind of *sechorah* or merchandise from the *B'rit Chadeshah* that Messiah was supposed to deliver when he came. Here I am referring to literal translation of Isaiah 62:11: "Behold Yehovah has proclaimed to the ends of the earth: Say ye to the daughter of Zion: 'Behold your *Yeshuah* comes; behold his merchandise (or reward) is with him, and his works (or labor) are before his face."

When that happened, what had been faith in the essence of the *B'rit Chadeshah*, suddenly became *da'at*, knowledge and understanding through reason. At that moment I became fully aware that both the Old Testament and the New Testament were one Book, and that together they made up the *shalem*, the *completed Bible*.

With that knowledge, I gained an even greater reward, the awareness that I now possessed several more pieces to the puzzle of our Lord's "Plan of Peace."

I now possessed the *neum Yehovah*, the guarantee of our Father, as recorded by our Prophets, whose every letter and word will last forever, that those scholars who insist that the Old and New Testaments are one complete Bible are indeed teachers of truth. I also knew in my heart that this complete Bible "is a Tree of Life to all who grasp it, and they that uphold it become enriched. Its ways are ways of pleasantness, and all its paths lead to peace" (Proverbs 3:17-18).

As I read the *B'rit Chadeshah* in Hebrew, a number of very important Hebrew words kept cropping up that clinched for me the fact that the *B'rit Chadeshah* is indeed a Jewish book.

The first word, and one the most important, was the Hebrew word *mechuyuv*, which connotes that the followers of Yehovah "have the responsibility" of doing our Father's will. From the time we were small children it was drummed into our heads that we were different than the *goyim*, the Gentiles. My father and the rabbis taught us that the *goyim* could do whatever their heads and hands wanted to do, but we must obey God's will and make this earth a better place for ourselves and future generations to live in. My father told us, "If we Jews don't make it, then the world won't make it. Then there will be another holocaust...."

As I read the *B'rit Chadeshah* in Hebrew, it dawned upon me that this word *mechuyuv* was used extensively, which was a clear indication that God had placed "responsibility" upon his chosen people to do his will.

The English word "faith" is *emunah* in Hebrew, which is the root word for "amen." The term denotes absolute faith in God's truth. *Emunah* means trust, reliance, full confidence in a promise. It means confidence or faith in truth, as opposed, for instance, to a Marxist who believes by faith that God is dead, without questioning the validity of his stand.

The Hebrew word *da'at* means "to know *by researching through reason.*" This is totally different than simply "thinking" or "feeling" something is so. Knowing comes from time spent investigating a precept or a subject with *Yehovah* (and allowing others to do the same). One "knows" his or her spouse by spending time and effort investigating, in researching (if these words will be allowed in this context), in learning to "know" that other person. An observant Jew "knows" Yehovah in this way, by seeking him, inquiring after him, investigating him in a deep, intimate, and thoroughgoing manner, which God blesses.

For example, each day when a male Jew puts on his *tallit* (prayer shawl), he prays, "Spread your lovingkindness upon those who *know* you" (Psalm 36:10). God honors such knowing by fulfilling his request. And when the male Jew puts on his *teffilin* (phylacteries), he does so in accordance with God's words to

Hosea: "And I will betroth thee unto me in faithfulness: and thou shalt *know* the Lord" (Hosea 2:22, v. 20
in English versions).

The word "grace," I have learned, is used many
times in the English Bible and seems to be a favorite
term, frequently spoken by Christians, though they
admit it is a difficult, perhaps even an impossible,
word to define. In Hebrew the word "grace" is *chesed,*
which means fairness, goodness, godliness. The noun
form is *chasid* and describes one who is fair and
square with God and his fellow man. For instance,
"Yehovah is just in all his ways and *chasid* (fair, good)
in all his doings" (Psalm 145:17).

Among the many Hebrew idioms used in both
the Old and New Testaments, a favorite of the Apostle
Paul is *chalilla,* which means "God forbid!" or "It is
impossible for God to have planned such a thing!"
Much of my confusion with the *B'rit Chadeshah*
or New Testament had to do with the fact that the
English versions, with strangely indefinable words (to
me, as well as to many Christians) and different cultural concepts, were at variance with my Hebrew
upbringing and understanding.

But all of this changed when I turned to my
Hebrew New Testament. The fuzziness and confusion

ceased to exist, and the New Testament became for me, which it actually is, an extension of the Old.

Other cultural and historical differences also bothered me, such as the move by the Roman Catholic Church in the fifth century to rule the world. The centuries following that alliance between Rome and the Church were dark years for the Jews, resulting in the Crusades and the Spanish Inquisition. In each of these historically documented institutions, Jews were persecuted, hunted down, tortured for their faith, and forced to convert under threat of sword or noose.

I could not understand (nor do I yet understand) why the Church excommunicated the Jewish believers in *Yeshuah* and forbade these Jews from the religious practices which Jesus himself followed. The best examples of these prohibitions are the *seder* dinner at Passover, other Jewish feasts, High Holy Days, and the practice of circumcision. The power of tradition is clearly demonstrated by the Passover *seder* service in Jewish homes everywhere. Even the least observant Jews heed this night of feasting to commemorate the Exodus from Egypt.

These and other questions came to me and remained as I read the Gospels. Not until I began researching Rabbi Paul's book of Romans did I begin to find answers to these questions.

During all of those dreadful years, just as foretold by our Prophets, millions of Jews were driven from their homes and lands and seemed to disappear, just as the Ten Northern Tribes (the so-called "Ten Lost Tribes") had seemed to disappear and cease to exist. It seemed that God had "forgotten" them.

Could this actually be the case? I wondered. Could it be possible that God would forget his own people? "Not so," I read Rabbi Paul explain. To put it in Hebrew, "*Chalilla*, it is impossible that God would forget the Jews forever."

The truth of Paul's statement in the latter part of our twentieth century is becoming evident, because the prophecy that "the Jewish-Christians of Israel shall return" is coming to pass in our day. As they do, I believe they will successfully bridge the culture gap that for centuries has seemed to exist between the Old and New Testaments.

Now that it was clear to me that the New Testament was as Jewish as the Old Testament and that the New was an extension of the Old, *Yeshuah* began opening doors for me. I realized I had been in error in my earlier attempts to share my message of *Yeshuah ha Meshiach* with my friends and family.

Why was that so? First, because I wasn't yet personally ready. I hadn't researched the *B'rit Chadeshah* enough for it to become as much a part of me as was the Torah. Second, a principle as important as the first, because our Lord had other work for me to do.

For example, because of my broad biblical Jewish background, I was given opportunity to advise the Beverly Hills Ahavat Zion Messianic Synagogue of their biblical rights in a controversy with another facet of Judaism. This resulted in an invitation to become Associate Rabbi for the Ahavat Zion Yeshivah. Most certainly, one of the "fringe benefits" of this association was that it brought me into contact with Bob Owen, with whom I co-authored this book. During this same time I was invited to become rabbi for the Notzrei Yisrael (Preservers of Israel) Synagogue in a nearby city.

I sometimes liken myself to both John the Baptist and the Apostle Paul. Like John the Baptist, as I attempted to take the Gospel to the Jews first, I considered myself a "voice crying in the wilderness." Similarly to the Apostle Paul, after spending years in my "Arabia," many doors of ministry were suddenly flung open wide. And, as both John the Baptist and the Apostle Paul had done, I entered all of those doors with great joy.

The *B'rit Chadeshah* became for me both a new land of discovery and a training ground. In it I discovered our Lord's blueprint for his Plan of Peace. And I learned how to prepare for spiritual battle in a field that was new territory for me.

As I opened the *B'rit Chadeshah* in Hebrew and began devouring its pages filled with the life-giving water, I became as thirsty as a camel after a desert trek. I simply could not drink enough.

CHAPTER ELEVEN
ADVENTURING WITH THE
APOSTLE PAUL

During my abortive attempts to read the
New Testament in English, I had picked up and
examined the Apostle Paul's Epistle to the Romans
several times. But without exception the Apostle's
language and concepts, at least in English, proved to
be an insurmountable barrier to me. However, as I
mentioned, when I began reading the New Testament
in Hebrew, *all of it* came alive, especially Rabbi Paul's
Epistle to the Romans.

In fact, the entire Book became so meaningful
to me, a new Jewish believer in the Messiah, that I
noted truths that should be familiar to all Christians.
However, in my contacts and relationships with
Christians, I noticed that many of these truths were as
unfamiliar (or undecipherable) to them as they had
been to me. One reason for this is that since the
Apostle was also a Jew, he and I share much of the

same background in Jewish culture, history, and language. But since the majority of Christians have none of that background, much of what the Apostle was saying is unclear or incomprehensible to them.

For example, anyone who is familiar with a *bet hamidrash* quickly realizes that Paul's Epistle to the Romans is a *midrash,* a teaching addressed to both Jews and non-Jews in a Jewish synagogue somewhere in Rome.

If a person had never been involved in a *bet hamidrash* dialogue, he might have some diffulty following Rabbi Paul's reasoning. But as the Apostle himself advised, with the understanding that Rabbi Paul was a follower of the One who is "the Way, the Truth, and the Light," the reader of this book must be prepared to take Paul's "pearls of wisdom" by faith.

Another prerequisite in studying Romans is to remember that our Father Yehovah gave instructions to *Yeshuah,* which he in turn passed on to Paul, and through him to each believer. Then we are to publish his Good News "to the ends of the earth." This is basically what the Apostle Paul is teaching.

With this in mind, I will show you what I believe Romans is saying to all those who seriously follow the Messiah. Paul's *midrash,* his teaching letter, is addressed to "all who are beloved of God in Rome, called as saints."

In other words, to all the followers of God in Rome, Rabbi Paul declared that his responsibility, personally delegated to him by *Yeshuah,* who appointed him to be an apostle, was to spread the light of Torah "to the Greeks, the forsaken, the wise and the foolish." Paul explained that the Jewish religious leaders knew they bore the responsibility to be a light to the world, yet they rebelled against the Living God, as had been prophesied. Nevertheless, Paul and a minority of the Jews accepted this responsibility and went out to spread the Gospel to the world.

Paul warns his audience of Jews and Romans not to do evil by violating the law, "Judge not lest ye be judged," because everyone receives his just rewards. Whether one was born a Jew or a Greek makes no difference to God. "He is not a respecter of persons." He will judge impartially. Whether a Jew sins by violating Torah, or a non-Jew by violating the admonition, "Do not judge," both are equally guilty.

The same principle applies to circumcision. Paul was saying that both the circumcised and the uncircumcised must obey "the spirit of Torah." Both must circumcise their hearts in order to obey the spirit of

Torah. Even though the Jew had been circumcised in the flesh, this inward circumcision applied to him as much as it did to the non-Jew. None were exempt from this fundamental truth.

Based on this foundational premise, the Apostle Paul asked the question that has bothered both Jews and non-Jews for centuries: Is there any benefit or advantage in being a Jew? And part of that same question is: What is the benefit of circumcision?

There is great advantage in being "of the circumcision," the Apostle said. First and foremost because it was to the "circumcision," to the Jews, that God entrusted his words, his blessed oracles.

Paul's statement reemphasized to me (as had my extensive research in Torah), that we Jews *have been given* the responsibility of being Yehovah's light-bearers to the world. God originally entrusted us with this task. For this reason, if for no other, Jews must keep their identity and must not fail to perform this tremendous commission.

Speaking as a Jew, the Apostle Paul asked his readers, "So, then, what if some Jews do not believe...?" Believe what? The question is more accurately translated, "What if some Jews were unfaithful in their responsibility to be light-bearers?" The Apostle was asking,

"What if some Jews were unfaithful to their God-given assignment? Would the fact of their unfaithfulness nullify or negate the faithfulness of God?"

"*Chalilla!*" Paul said. "God forbid, it can never be!" As I carefully read the Apostle's letter, especially his statement that it is every believer's responsibility (both Jew and non-Jew) to keep the spirit of Torah by accepting the inward circumcision of the heart, a new thought came to me. If the principle of spiritual heart circumcision applied to both Jews and non-Jews, then *the Apostle must also be saying that the responsibility of spreading the light, the Gospel, the Good News, is also the co-responsibility of both Jews and non-Jews!*

Could this actually be what the Apostle Paul was saying? I had to be sure. I read and reread Paul's writings, examining them from every angle, from every viewpoint. Finally I came to the conclusion that Paul was actually saying: *God is not only the God of the Jews,* but of the uncircumcised as well. The *goyim,* the Gentiles, could also be witnesses of God's righteousness through *emunah* or faith in God's truth.

This was dynamite!

"And those who come to God through faith in his truth," Paul asked, "do they nullify Torah? *Chililla!* God forbid! On the contratry; they uphold Torah" (3:31).

I could scarcely believe what I was reading! But it was clear, the Apostle Paul was saying that God is the God of both the Jews and the Gentiles, and *it is acceptable to come to him either by Torah or by faith*. This was a staggering new truth to me.

Though my growing familiarity with Christians and their (to me) strange theology, I realized that the majority of Christians strongly believed that one could only come to God and *Yeshuah* by faith. While I as a Jew, on the other hand, had always been taught that one must come to God through his intellectual comprehension of God in Torah. Now this Rabbi Paul was teaching that one could come to God either way. Both ways were perfectly valid.

This was strong medicine, very difficult for me to accept. But Paul verified his conclusions in chapter 4 where he stated that since Abraham came to believe in God through faith (v. 13), Christ's disciples must hold to the same faith as Abraham to be reckoned righteous just as Abraham was (v. 16). I leaned back and meditated upon what I had read. The more I thought about the Apostle's conclusions, the more I realized that I could not fault his reasoning.

Again and again, as I read Paul's *midrash* to the Romans, I had to keep reminding myself that the one who wrote it, the one who continually spoke of victory and who forcefully declared that "nothing can separate us from the love of God which is in Jesus Christ our Lord!"—this man was a Jewish rabbi! This was something else the two of us had in common. I also had to remember that Rabbi Paul was as totally orthodox as it was possible for a Jew to be.

Despite these facts, as I continued my research into the *B'rit Chadeshah,* I became increasingly aware that there are no stronger statements regarding the lordship of *Yeshuah ha Meshiach,* Jesus the Messiah, to be found in the entire Bible than those made in the writings of this Rabbi Paul. As I soaked myself in the Epistle to the Romans, my admiration for the writer increased by the hour. I marveled at his intimate familiarity with Torah, which is evident as he skillfully drew from it at will to validate his message.

I soon realized how crucial it is that both Jews and Christians understand what Rabbi Paul was saying. From my own rabbinical viewpoint, I certainly was able to appreciate the "risk" (if I might be permitted to use the term in this regard) Paul took in fearlessly preaching these hitherto unrevealed truths: *one,* that God has chosen *both* the Jews and the followers of Messiah. And, *two,* that they are now equally responsible to him to be his light-bearers to the world.

Though the Apostle Paul hoped that his teaching would not alienate him from Judaism, Paul went on to say that not everyone who is born a Jew remains a Jew, because "the children of the flesh" must also become "the children of promise" if they are to be counted as Abraham's "seeds" or descendants. Therefore, Paul stated, God will call some from the Jews and others from the Gentiles (Romans 9:24).

If I correctly understood the Apostle's conclusions, it meant that with my recognition of the Messiahship of *Yeshuah*, I, Orthodox Rabbi Isidor Zwirn, was now automatically a part of an eternal alliance with Christians to help bring my unbelieving Jewish compatriots to Messiah!

CHAPTER TWELVE
GOD IS ALIVE AND WELL

For several years I continued my studies in both the Old and New Testaments, learning more and more about God's great Plan of Peace which he longs to impart to all of his creatures.

One morning, as I was deep in my research, the phone rang. "Rabbi Zwirn," an unfamiliar voice began, "I'd like to come and spend some time talking with you."

On the appointed day, my visitor arrived at my office. We chatted for a while about his great interest in Jewish things, then agreed to meet again. A week or so later when he arrived, he had a book in his hand and a troubled look on his face.

After the amenities were over, he handed me the book. Though I knew of the author, I had not seen the book. "The book has sold hundreds of thousands," my visitor told me. "The writer talks about God's impotence instead of his omnipotence. He writes of God's inability to answer the prayers of those who cry unto him, or to meet their needs."

I shrugged. "There are many books like that."

"Not quite like this one," he said. "This one was written by a man of God, by a Jewish rabbi."

That caught my attention. I opened the book and began leafing through it.

"I'd like you to read it," my friend said. "I'll come back in a few days and we'll talk about it."

By the time he had returned, I had read the book and made extensive notes. When my friend seated himself I picked up the book.

"Did you read it?" he asked.

I nodded. "Yes, I read it through."

"What do you think about it?"

"I think someone should write a counter to his claims of his too-weak God, about his God who is powerless to help his hurting children."

"I agree," he said.

We were silent for a moment or so, both of us seemingly gripped by the same thought. I spoke first.

"Let's write it," I said impulsively.

He smiled and nodded. "Let's do."

And so we began.

Though Bob Owen is not a Jew, he has a Jewish heart, and he believes as I do that God and his Word are truly alive and full of power. We believe that only the Bible can make one wise. Only the Bible can lead us and provide peace and power and hope. This is because only the Bible has "the words of life."

To neglect or ignore the Bible is to turn from the Tree of Life. To reject the Bible is to reject life and the Author of Life. Yehovah said, "Take to your heart all the words with which I am warning you today, which you shall command your sons to observe carefully, even all the words of this law. For it is not an idle word for you; indeed it is your life. And by this word you shall prolong your days" (Deuteronomy 32:46, 47).

"I call heaven and earth to witness against you today," says Yehovah, "that I have set before you life and death, the blessing and the curse. So choose life in order that you may live, you and your descendants, by loving the Lord your God, by obeying his voice, and by holding fast to him; for this is your life and the length of your days" (Deuteronomy 30:19, 20).

This "life" God is referring to is the Bible. Only the Bible can reveal to us Yehovah, his creativity, his works, and his wonders. Only the Bible can reveal to us the magnificence and glory of our God.

And all of this enormous store of truth, knowledge, and life starts with Yehovah's very first words to mankind: "In the beginning *Elohim barah...*" *Elohim,* the Spirit of God; *barah,* "to essence," "to give purpose to."

On that day of beginnings, when Yehovah spoke, the entire physical earth was in chaos and disorder. The Spirit of God (1) gave each unit its essence or purpose, (2) planned every detail of the new creation, and (3) made, manufactured, or brought into being that new creation.

Then, when the physical universe was complete, Yehovah crowned his creative masterpiece by making mankind in his own *tzelem* (likeness). I am continually amazed that all of mankind, you and I, are actually "made in his image," his "likeness"! But how can I know what that means unless I know Yehovah, unless I understand him? The obvious answer is, "I cannot."

Well, then, who is Yehovah?

Our Jewish *Shema* speaks that question very well, because the centrality of a Jew's faith rests upon the essence of Yehovah as stated in the *Shema,* our credal declaration. If this eternal truth were to be proven false, then the Bible and Yehovah would be meaningless and would fade from the scene.

The *Shema* is the first spiritual lesson a child is taught, and the last words uttered by or spoken in the hearing of the dying. The *Shema* has come from the lips of countless martyrs who refused to deny their Jewishness.

In Hebrew, the *Shema* is transliterated: *Shema, Yisrael, Adonai Elohenu, Adonai echad."*

Translated into English, the *Shema* declares, "Hear, O Israel, Adonai, Yehovah is our God. And this God is the One and all of life."

Yehovah is the one living God who governs all, knows all, gave essence to all, directs all, and owns all. He is the only perfect One who is omnipotent, omniscient, and omnipresent. He is also anthropomorphic, for he is composed of all the physical units which include every eye, every ear, every hand, every bodily part and unit of the universe!

What about Yehovah, with all these attributes? Is he near when I need him? Does he know me? Does he see me? Does he care about me? When I hurt, will he minister to me? When I am ill or injured, can he heal me? Will he come to my assistance when I am frightened or lonely? Will he protect me from harm and danger?

Yes...*yes*...YES! For he sent us his messenger

(Malachi 3:1), whose name is *Yeshuah,* to prove that he loves us, that he cares for us. He has prepared the best kind of government for us, installing his own Son and Messenger as ruler over it.

Adonai Yehovah ("Lord God," a term used frequently throughout the Bible), is never too busy, never too distant, never weak, never asleep, never forgetful.

Adonai Yehovah is alive and well.

Adonai Yehovah is alive and full of power.

Adonai Yehovah has not changed.

Though some of his rebellious children have spoken ill of him, he is still the same.

Though some of his rebellious children have deserted him, his power, his influence, his control are not diminished.

He is *Adonai Yehovah,* our Father, the one Living God of the universe. And he is perfectly able to handle his own affairs and the affairs of this vast universe.

Yehovah is as able to handle the affairs of his vast empire as he ever was. Nothing about him has weakened or dissipated. He is the same powerful, yet loving God he has always been. Nothing about him has changed. He is the same as he has always been. And always will be.

Yehovah revealed himself to his chosen eternal

family of Israel through Abraham, and he did this by offering Abraham a "good deal." That good deal is spelled out in detail in Genesis 12:1-3.

Basically Yehovah's deal with Abraham was initiated by his spoken Word when he said to Abraham, "Leave the land of your birth and go to a Promised Land that I am going to show you." In so speaking, Yehovah offered Abraham a rich contract or covenant. And what was that promise or contract?

Yehovah said, "I will make you into a great nation, and I will bless you, and I will make your name great." That was God's part of the contract.

But what about Abraham? What was his part of the deal?

Abraham's responsibility, his part in the contract, is expressed in two Hebrew words: "*Veheyeh Beracha*," "Be a blessing." Yehovah simply told Abraham to be a blessing.

Even before Abraham had time to respond to God's generous offer, God sweetened the deal. "I will bless those that bless you," he said, "and I will curse them that curse you." Actually, what better deal could a Jew, or anyone, ask for?

Knowing the *chutzpah* (intrinsic nature) of Israel, I'm certain that Abraham must have asked of Yehovah,

"What do you mean, 'Become a blessing?' To whom am I to become a blessing? To myself? Or to others? Explain what you mean."

Yehovah answered, "Be a blessing to both yourself and to others. For I want you to act as a role model for all of my children."

My father and other Orthodox Jews explained God's statement in this way: Jews were to live like goldfish in a glass jar. "Because," my father told me, "everything a Jew does is being continually observed by our Creator. Furthermore, everything we do is also observed by all the families on the earth."

He explained that if we did our Father's will and thus "blessed our lives," no matter how unwise, how profligate the *goyim* were, they would soon begin living as we did because they would see the rich rewards we were receiving from our Father. Then they would begin emulating our life-style.

After all, who doesn't want to live a blessed life?

But, then, you may be asking the same question I asked. "Why did Yehovah offer Abraham such a good deal in the first place?"

CHAPTER THIRTEEN
WHY DID GOD GIVE ABRAHAM SUCH A GOOD DEAL?

That's a very good question. Why did he?

I'll give you the same answer I got. Up till and including the time in which Abraham lived, the whole earth lived by what might be called the morality of the jungle: might is right. Every city was a state unto itself. To prevent the encroachments of its neighboring city-states, each city-state was forced to build a high wall around its own city.

Between these city-state kingdoms a condition of continuous war existed. Each was out to "protect" his own rights and boundaries and at the same time "enlarge" his own holdings. There could be no relaxation of vigilance by any of these little kingdoms.

There was no exception to this rule. You either conquered them or they conquered you. Sometimes two, three, or even four of these little kingdoms would form a temporary alliance to conquer other such alliances. But they soon broke up until one giant city-state would take over the then-known world, which we now know as the "Fertile Crescent." Then, when that huge, formidable state became strong enough, it would attack the giant southern state of Egypt or be attacked by it.

The results of these battles were always the same. The conquered became the slaves of the conqueror. And because the gods of the conquerors were considered also to be stronger than those of the vanquished peoples, the victor's priesthood would also take over the loser's priesthood and install the "stronger" gods over the entire area. This practice continued well into the period of Rome's rulership of the entire known world.

Looking at the Bible, we can better recognize the problems that faced the kings of Israel. With which of the super-powers were they to align themselves? The problem was not just their own, but was shared by the smaller states that were caught in the super-powers' struggles for supremacy.

Picking the winner of winners became the problem that had to be faced and handled by our prophets.

From the dawn of history, this situation existed throughout the world. But Yehovah had other plans for his chosen people. Thus came the big change.

Clearly, a new type of society was needed. For reasons known only to himself, Yehovah chose Abraham to become the founding father of a just and peace-loving society. With the founding of the society headed by Abraham, history began its change from a barbaric to a more civilized culture.

Following Abraham's beginning, to Moses was handed down the law by which this new social order was to be directed. This was named the First Covenant. The rest of the struggle is told to us by our prophets in the Torah.

Now, what is the difference between the First and the Second Covenants? The First was offered to just two nations that emerged from Abraham, the Arabs and the Israelites. The eldest sons, Ishmael and Esau, rejected the "big deal" offer. But the same offer was accepted by the younger sons, Isaac and Jacob. The Second Covenant of Jesus, also called the Covenant of Peace, has been offered to *all of our Father's children*. In Christ there is "neither Jew nor Greek (non-Jew), black or white, male or female."

The similarity between the Old and New Covenants

is that *all* of "the recipients are to be blessed." The Old Covenant required obedience to the laws of Torah. The New Covenant requires obedience to "the spirit of Torah" *and* the laws of love of our Lord. In the end, Rabbi Paul claimed, the results will be exactly the same.

What are the results that are guaranteed by both covenants? That's also a good question.

Basically, it boils down to the fact that Yehovah always intended that his children were to be happy and prosperous. He intended that they should be healthy and happy and full of peace. Jesus was the epitome and model of these intentions and plans of God, for Jesus "went about doing good, and healing all...for God was with him" (Acts 10:38).

Despite Jesus' modeling of God's intentions for all his children, "yet they (the multitudes) were not (all) believing in him" (John 12:37). This was so, in order that the prophecy of Isaiah would be fulfilled, "Lord, who has believed our report? And to whom has the arm of the Lord been revealed?" (Isaiah 53:1). Because of this disparity, it became possible for the *goyim* who were willing to bless themselves by researching Torah to enter the stage of history and become the light of the world.

We have all heard a common proverb that challenges, "Physician, heal yourself," meaning that the same medicine or treatment a doctor uses on his patient should be effective enough to heal the doctor too. This is true of our Father. He is in the best of health, because his medicine is the best. Our Father is our Great Physician. His Word is the best medicine in the world, because it is "for the healing of the nations" (Revelation 22:2).

Yehovah made it clear for anyone who has sinned and lived far from him, even the Egyptians, that when they "return unto the Lord, he...will heal them" (Isaiah 19:22), for, "by his stripes we shall be healed" (Isaiah 53:5). Even though they may have closed their eyes and ears to the truth of God's Word, the moment any sinning or rebellious person or nation returns to him, *they will be healed.* (Acts 28:28 is an affirmation of Isaiah 6:10.)

Jesus said, "Blessed are the peacemakers." And how right he was, for the peacemakers are truly blessed. God says in Isaiah 57:19 that those who create fruits of peace with their mouths will be healed.

So, through obedience to his Word, our Father has put within each of us the ability to bring healing to our own situations. He has told us that every letter, every word, every promise in his Word is true, that *it cannot fail.*

He has told us that his Word "is a tree of life to those who take hold of her...that all of her ways are peace...and happy are those who uphold her" (Proverbs 3:17, 18).

That *tree of life* was in the Garden of Eden (Genesis 2:9) and it is in the New Jerusalem (Revelation 22:2). God tells us that every leaf (every letter and every word) of that tree brings healing to all who will take upon themselves the yoke of the Kingdom of God. Jesus spoke of that yoke, saying, "My yoke is easy and...light" (Matthew 11:29).

This means that God's Word is the medicine that will meet every single one of our needs.

Does God care about his children? Yes, he does.

Is God able to do anything about fear and pain? Yes.

Is God able to protect his children from harm and evil? Yes.

Does God cause bad things to happen to good people? No, he does not.

Does God cause good things to happen to good people when they research his Word, hide it in their hearts, and let their light shine for all to see? Yes, he most certainly does.

How does he do this?

God says, "My son, attend to my Word, consent and submit to my sayings. Let them not depart from your sight. Keep them in the center of your heart. For they (my words) are life to those who find them, healing and health (and protection and prosperity) to their whole body" (Proverbs 4:20-22).

This means that God's words themselves contain the essence of God; therefore, *when we are filled with God's Word,* we are filled with God himself. And we know that in God there is no pain or suffering or sickness.

"The entrance of thy Word bringeth light" (Psalm 119:130).

"The Word that God speaks is alive and full of power, making it active, operative, energizing, and effective" (Hebrews 4:16).

"He sent his Word and healed them and delivered them from all their destructions" (Psalm 107:20).

These and hundreds of other Scriptures like them show us that when we, as children of God, are continuously being filled with his Word and are living according to the dictates of that Word, then we have the power actually dwelling *within ourselves* to promote healing for every situation.

A good example of this is to be found in

Deuteronomy 28:1-14, which begins: "If you will *shamaw* or listen diligently to the voice of the Lord your God (God's Word is his voice), being watchful *to do* all his commandments which I command you this day, the Lord your God will set you high above all the nations of the earth, and *all these blessings shall come upon you* and overtake you, if you heed the voice of the Lord your God" (vv. 1-12).

What follows, spelled out in verses 3-13, is the essence of all God's goodness to his children. He promises superabundant prosperity in every realm of life. The condition, however, is the *hearing* and the *doing* of all God's commandments.

The rest of chapter 28 lists in great detail all the pains, suffering, sickness, problems, and death that most certainly *will come* to those who "will not obey the voice of the Lord your God, being watchful to do all his commandments and his statutes" for which he holds us responsible.

Perhaps God's promise to heal every problem, sickness, and circumstance that could possibly come upon his children can best be summed up by his words to Moses, "If you will diligently hearken to the voice of the Lord your God, and will do what is right in his sight, and will listen to and obey his commandments and keep all his statutes, *I will put none of the diseases upon you which I brought upon the Egyptians,* for I am the Lord who heals you" (Exodus 15:26).

So God is not unconcerned about us.

God is not powerless to help.

He is not blind or deaf to our needs and our cries.

He has made provision to provide and care for us in every detail of life.

God rewards the righteous with good:

"Blessed is the man that walketh not in the council of the ungodly, nor standeth in the way of the sinners, nor sitteth in the seat of the scornful. But his delight is in the Torah of the Lord; and in his Torah doth he meditate day and night. And he shall be like a tree planted by the rivers of water that bringeth forth his fruit in his season; his leaf also shall not wither, and *whatsoever he doeth* shall prosper" (Psalm 1:1-3).

The reward of the wicked is his own doing.

"The ungodly are not so; but are like the chaff which the wind driveth away....For the Lord knoweth the way of the righteous (concerns himself with the righteous, so that he prospers); but the way of the ungodly shall perish" (vv. 4-6).

The bottom line is that God does not act in an

unpredictable, whimsical manner. He does not capriciously heap bad things upon good people. He rewards good people with good things. He is the God of righteousness. "Just and good is he."

However, he is the God of justice, fairness, rightness. He has standards of righteousness by which he lives, standards by which he expects us all to live. Those who persistently refuse to abide by those standards suffer. *It isn't that they "break the law of God," so much as they "break themselves upon the laws of God."*

Heal thyself? Be your own physician? Yes.

Yes, in the sense that the "medication" is available. So is the prescription for taking it. By following the directions that have been laid out in God's Word, the "medication" works. If the directions are not followed closely, the medication will work only some of the time, to some degree. But it is the privilege of God's children to obey his Word and live in health, safety, happiness and peace. Shalom!

God made a good deal with Abraham, that he has extended to all of his children. It is spelled out in God's communication with Abraham, and confirmed throughout both the Old and New Covenants:

"Bless yourselves," God said to Abraham (and to all

of his obedient children), "*and I will bless you. Be a blessing to yourselves and to all those around you. And I will bless you with my shalom, my totally comprehensive peace, happiness, health, and prosperity.*"

That is a good deal!

וַיֵּצֵא הַחֹתָם מִגַּנְ יֶשְׁיִנְצִגר מִשַּׁרְשָׁיו יִפְרֶה

EPILOGUE
THE MEETING AND MERGING OF TWO
CULTURES *by the coauthor, Bob Owen*

Setting: Santa Monica Pier.

Occasion: One cool Sunday afternoon.

Characters: Thousands of sightseers and a single man.

Plot: None.

That Sunday afternoon on the pier I met two single, elderly ladies. The meeting was brief, but it profoundly affected my life and the life of my family.

One lady was sitting by herself on a bench watching the sea gulls and the ocean. I sat down and struck up a conversation with her. Apparently I looked harmless enough, so she chatted pleasantly with me, that is, until I asked her, "Do you know Jesus?"

She spoke sharply. "I am of a different religion!"

"Oh," I said, "and what is it?"

"I am a Jew."

Before I could reply the second lady walked up and asked, "Dorothy, you look upset. What's the matter?"

Dorothy pulled herself to the very end of the bench.

"This man believes in Jesus."

The newcomer said, "So do I."

Dorothy was shocked. "But you're a Jew!"

"So was Jesus."

Michal, the second lady, was a Jewish believer! Instantly there was a warm kinship between the two of us. As we chatted briefly she told me about her "Messianic synagogue," a term I had never heard. "Come and visit us," She said. A week or so later my wife and I took advantage of her invitation.

We arrived a few minutes early and a prayer meeting was going on. People were praying in the name of *Yeshuah ha Meshiach*. Since that memorable evening my family and I have developed a close kinship with a number of those Jewish believers. And a few months ago we attended our first *yeshivah*.

I didn't know what to expect, but I didn't have long to wait. The small group consisted of about an equal number of Jews and Christians. At the appointed time the teaching rabbi began with the announcement, "This is a *bet hamidrash....*"

It was a new term to me, but I soon understood it.

Is it possible for Jews and Christians to come together in a *bet hamidrash?* Is it possible for Jews and Christians to come together for any purpose?

Is it possible for these two traditionally distinct and different cultures to come together for the purpose of researching God's Word in the spirit of love, understanding, and humility? To find it mutually beneficial in doing so?

Five years ago I would have said, "No way."

Today I say, "Certainly."

Five years ago, I must admit, I had never known a Jew, much less had a meaningful conversation with one. In my Merchant Marine days I had sailed with a young Jewish cadet, but had never more than passed the time of day with him.

Five years ago my total knowledge of Jews and Judaism could have been summed up by two cliches: "*They* came from Israel," and, "*They* rejected Jesus." I literally knew nothing about Jewish culture or Jewish history. And though I had prepared for the ministry, I couldn't tell an *aleph* from a *tav*.

Today I know much more, but not nearly enough. I do know that the roots of Christianity are buried deeply in Judaism and that the Bible is a Jewish Book. All of its writers were Jews, with the possible exception of Luke, who was probably a Jewish proselyte. The majority of the Bible was originally written in Hebrew and all of the early followers of Jesus were Jews.

And, probably most important of all, Jesus was a Jew.

What's more, he was a Jewish rabbi. Though some of his contemporaries accused him of disloyalty to their religion, scholarly research gives him a clean slate. He never violated biblical law. By his own admission, he came to uphold it.

And, whatever else he came to earth to accomplish, he avowedly came to unite mankind, "That they might be one," he prayed to his Father, "as we are one."

The Apostle Paul (Rabbi Paul) declared that Jesus came to be "our peace...(and to make) both groups (Jews and non-Jews) into one...(by breaking) down the barrier of the dividing wall...that in himself he might make the two into one new man, thus establishing peace" (Ephesians 2:14-15).

During these past several years, I have become intimately involved with the Jewish community. My wife and daughter have both worked as secretaries for a Jewish synagogue. We have attended numerous synagogues, both traditional and Messianic. Our youngest son has spent a year in Israel studying the history, culture, language, and geography of that land and people. We are all involved in various levels of Hebrew language study.

Now, for the question again:

Is it possible for Jews and Christians to come together in a meaningful way to *doresh* (research) the Bible in a *bet hamidrash* manner?

The answer is yes.

Is it possible for Christians to begin dialoguing with Jews about the Jews' own Bible? The answer is yes.

I am seeing it happen. Not on a large scale yet, but it is a beginning, a significant beginning. And it's very, very exciting!

Is it possible for Christians to make the Jews jealous of their position and relationship with God? Jealous enough for those Jews to come back to Yehovah? Again the answer is yes. But it won't be easy. It will be difficult at first, because it will take time, discipline, commitment.

But Jesus himself said, "My yoke is easy and my burden is light."

You can start such a *bet hamidrash* yourself, right where you are—in your home or church, but following the principles outlined by Rabbi Zwirn.

It is truly exciting to be a part of such a meeting of these two cultures, to see how beautifully they can come together in the Spirit of our Lord. Furthermore, since I have become personally involved with my Jewish brethren, I have felt a new zest for life, a new awareness that all of his promises apply to me *without exception*.

This fact alone has enabled me to more fully appropriate the "power to shut up the mouths of our enemies and avengers" (Psalm 8:3), those enemies and powers that seek to destroy the friends and children of our Father.

As a result, I truly believe God's Word to us that we need never be afraid. And we need never be ashamed.

And I believe as I have never believed before that all of us who are followers of the Messiah must act upon the knowledge that our Lord Jesus demands of us, that *we are* the "light of the world," and live accordingly. I believe that we actually are and can become that light.

Furthermore, taught and undergirded by the *Ruach haemet*, the Spirit of Truth, I believe we can spread that light.

Let's do it!

Shalom!

Rabbi Isidor Zwirn was aglow and burning with the
Ruach Hakodesh (Spirit of God).

Rabbi Zwirn and coauthor Bob Owen.

The *tallit* or prayer shawl is worn in traditional synagogues by every male age 13 and older.

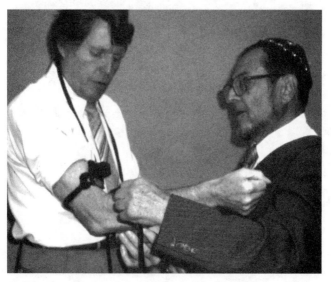

Rabbi Zwirn instructing Bob Owen in "laying *tefillin*." This set of *tefillin* owned by Rabbi Zwirn's grandfather was presented by Rabbi Zwirn to Bob Owen.

GLOSSARY

Adonai: our Lord. In English translations, often used synonymously for Yehovah, our Father. In Torah, *Adonai Yehovah* are used together to signify that they are one.

Barah: the first step in all creations. The word means "to give purpose or essence" to every part within the universe. *Yetzirah* is the second process, "to design." *Assiyah* is the last process of creation, "to make or manufacture." Throughout Torah each of these words is carefully used in the process of creation.

Bar mitzvah: literally, "son of the commandments." The ceremony marks the initiation of a 13-year-old boy into the Jewish religious community, by his acceptance of his responsibility to Torah's laws.

Bat mitzvah: exactly the same, except for young women.

Bet hamidrash: house of research, arrived at from the commandments of Torah.

B'rit Chadeshah: New Testament or New Covenant.

This was long ago prophesied as the agency that would create "a new heart and a new spirit."

Chalilla: "God forbid! It is unthinkable that God would plan or allow such a thing."

Chesed: equivalent to grace in the Gospel. In Hebrew it means fairness, goodness, and lovingkindness.

Da'at: knowing; to understand by objective knowledge.

Doresh: seek, study, research, investigate.

Echad: the only *one* that is also the *all*.

Elohim: in Torah is most often used as the Holy Spirit of the universe. Being plural, it sometimes means the perfect unity of *Adonai Yehovah*.

Emunah: has the same root as "amen." Denotes absolute belief in God's truth and unfailing goodness; and in his deliverance in times of distress. For Jews, the hopefulness for a better world.

Goy: (plural goyim): Gentile, heathen, non-Jew.

Havdalah: a prayer said in the synagogue at the

conclusion of the Sabbath evening service. The entire prayer speaks of "the God of my salvation."

Jew: in Hebrew, *Judah*. Anyone born of Jewish parents; one who embraces the Jewish way of life.

Kabbalah: the Jewish mystical book which researches the Holy Spirit of Elohim down to its finest details.

Kaddish: said immediately after researching a portion of Torah or Talmud. Also, an indirect prayer for the departed which embodies the Messianic hope, but contains no reference to the dead.

Kedosh Yisrael: a term used in Torah, as well as in the Jewish Daily Prayer Book. It is a special title given to the Messiah. Literally, "the Holiest One of Israel."

Law: in Hebrew specifically the Mosaic Law given at Sinai. In the New Testament it is invariably translated Torah.

Mechuyuv: responsibility to God. This is drummed into the heads of all *yeshivah* students.

Netzer: (verb) preserve, watch over, guard, Christianize.

Notzrei Yisrael: as used in Torah: guardians, protectors or Christians of Israel.

Notzrim: (also prophesied in Torah) Christians, preservers, watchmen, guardians.

Orthodox Judaism: branch of Judaism unchanged for the last 2,000 years in exile. It embraces the validity of Torah, but adds the rabbinic teachings to be as valid as Torah.

Prophets: The Hebrew word is *navi* and signifies a seer or spokesman for God. Prophets know that their words must stand forever, for if their words are false they will disappear from the earth.

Rabbi: a teacher of Torah. Is often the head of a congregation and is qualified to decide questions of Torah. In Europe rabbis were also judges of their community and the head of the "house of justice," the *bet din*.

Rebbetzin, or *rebitzin:* a rabbi's wife.

Ruach haemet: Spirit of Truth.

Shabbat—Sabbath: for Jews it begins twenty minutes before sundown Friday evening, and concludes when the first star appears in the sky Saturday evening.

Shalem: complete; that is, "completed Jew," "complete Bible."

Shema: literally, "Hear!" The *Shema* has been the keynote of Judaism throughout the ages. It proclaims the Oneness of God, which is to be followed by our love, loyalty, and promise to do his will. The English rendering is: "Hear, O Israel, the Lord is our God, the Lord is One."

Sinas chinum: unjust hatred, hatred without a cause.

Tanach: Jewish Bible or Old Testament. The word is an acronym, the letters of which stand for Torah, the Prophets, and other writings from the Bible.

Torah: literally, "to direct, point the way." The five Books of Moses, the Pentateuch; the scroll used in readings in the synagogue. Today used as synonymous to the Old Testament.

Tallit: four-cornered prayer shawl with fringes *(tzitzit).*

Tefillin: phylacteries in small leather cases containing the Shema. These are affixed to forehead and arm when praying.

Tzaddik: a righteous or just person. The verb is *tzadek.*

Weekly portion of Torah: the five Books of Moses, with corresponding readings from the Prophets (*Haftorah*); divided into fifty-two weekly portions to be read each year.

Yeshivah: traditional Hebrew school dedicated to the study of Torah and other rabbinic works; *bet hamidrash* principles used in study.

Yehovah or Jehovah: in Torah used exclusively for our Father.

Yeshuah: Hebrew for salvation; the One who will bring salvation, Jesus. Therefore, *Yeshuah ha Meshiach,* Jesus the Messiah, to Christians.